IT'S MY PLEASURE

IT'S MY PLEASURE

DECOLONIZING SEX POSITIVITY

MO ASEBIOMO

NEW DEGREE PRESS

COPYRIGHT © 2021 MO ASEBIOMO

IT'S MY PLEASURE

Decolonizing Sex Positivity

ISBN	978-1-63730-809-7	*Paperback*
	978-1-63730-871-4	*Kindle Ebook*
	978-1-63730-979-7	*Ebook*

To a younger me and to Ariel for helping me find her.

CONTENTS

PREFACE: A LETTER TO YOU

———

This book is a love letter to myself that I have been writing for years. It just so happens that the medium is this book, and that you, the reader, are privy to my journey of becoming and unbecoming.

My writing started and ended with this question: What kind of person did I need when I was younger? I ask myself this question when I am looking for direction in my life. What kind of person did I need, and what decisions would lead me closer to becoming that person now?

Throughout my childhood and adolescence, when it came to the topic of sex, I thought I was alone in my experience. I considered the sex-related thoughts in my head to be dirty. I was convinced it was perverse to be curious about bodies. I felt completely alone.

I decided to write this book at a time in my life when I felt so much shifting inside of me. I so desperately wanted to be a person that my younger self would admire, love and be proud of, but the list of things I needed to learn to get to that place was overwhelming and daunting. Regret was a close companion of mine:

I wish I had learned this. I wish I could have known that. My life would be so different if someone had mentored me about these things.

And so on.

These questions and regrets were drenched in shame until I started writing and ultimately traded that shame for curiosity. Shame is heavy. It bogs us down and enshrouds us in regret. Curiosity is much lighter. Friendlier. Safer.

When we lead with curiosity, we can learn more about ourselves and the world around us. Perhaps if we taught that it was normal and healthy to be curious about sex, sexuality, gender, and everything in between, we all would not have so much to unlearn.

SEX EDUCATION AND PHOTOSYNTHESIS

During the peak of the COVID-19 pandemic, I found myself in the same corner of the universe as a dear friend of mine, Vinh Ton. We had met in college and continued to live together in the last months of 2020, brushing our teeth while dancing and swapping stories while stargazing. Vinh was my first real interview for the book. As a first-generation queer man of Vietnamese descent, his voice and stories had to be captured in my writing. Since Vinh's interview, I went on to talk to all sorts of people who live, work, and exist in the intersections of sexuality, race, and identity. Throughout my interviews, I noticed a pattern in the stories I heard. Whether it was from sexuality educators, sex workers, psychologists, or friends of mine, many of our first experiences of sex education sounded a lot like the story Vinh shared.

Vinh says, "Learning about sex at my school was like learning about how plants go through photosynthesis. It was purely biological and existed in a vacuum as only procreation between a man and a woman. It did little to acknowledge the multitude of ways that sex can happen or best practices with sex."

Vinh and I both grew up in the South. I spent most of my adolescence in South Georgia and Vinh was raised in Charleston, South Carolina. In our interview, Vinh told me about the day in high school when the boys and girls in his class were separated and taken to different rooms to learn about sex. As Vinh tells his story, I envision a dimly lit room, an overhead projector and images of penises and pubic hair. I imagine thinly veiled coughs masking laughter and snickering. I picture Vinh, quiet—absorbing his teacher's words and the reactions of his classmates.

Vinh says, "I can't speak on how the girls were socialized within these programs in South Carolina, but for the boys, the notion of pleasure was embedded as if it was a natural biological fact." In other words, sex was taught with the assumption and expectation that those with a penis would experience pleasure simply as a byproduct of sexual intercourse.

He continues, "I'm not sure if the girls in the other classroom were taught the same thing. Like if their pleasure was also included in this biological function of sex or if they were just co-opted into it."

Our first lessons of sex can be very powerful, even if that lesson is nonexistent. The demonstration of silence or the absence of sex education is a statement in and of itself.

I know that my own sex education was not nearly as complete as it should have been. During my freshman year in a public high school in South Georgia, my class and I completed a worksheet that instructed us to define different sexually transmitted infections. After that, we were offered an abstinence pledge. Anyone who signed the pledge would be awarded bonus points on their gym class average. I did not hesitate to sign that piece of paper.

A 104% average for gym class? Why would I pass that up?

Needless to say, the words "pleasure" or "orgasm" were never mentioned. Many of my peers and colleagues recount similar experiences.

THE LANDSCAPE OF SEX EDUCATION
In the United States, there are three main types of sex education:
1. Abstinence Only Sex Education
2. Abstinence Plus Education
3. Comprehensive Curriculum

Natalie Blanton from the University of Utah summarizes these main types of education in her article "Why Sex Education in the United States Needs an Update and How to Do It."

Abstinence Only and Abstinence Only Until Marriage Programs are sometimes called Sexual Risk Avoidance Programs. These types of curricula emphasize abstinence as the most effective and moral approach for youth and teenagers. (*Abstinence* means someone is abstaining or choosing not to have sex altogether.)

Abstinence Only curriculum does not typically provide information or training about contraception or safe and healthy ways to engage in sex.

Abstinence Plus Education covers information about contraception and condoms while still promoting abstinence until marriage.

On the other hand, Comprehensive Sex Education teaches students that sexuality is normal and healthy. It seeks to do so by covering an array of topics including relationships, interpersonal skills, consent, and sexual health (Blanton 2019).

Blanton says the following about the effects of comprehensive sex education.

> *Comprehensive sex education helps young people delay sexual intercourse, increases condom and contraceptive use, and reduces the number of partners. When teens do choose to become sexually active, this curriculum decreases the likelihood and frequency of unprotected*

sex. Furthermore, students who learn from a version of comprehensive sex-ed that includes gay, lesbian, and transgender issues report a safer school environment with less bullying and harassment. Despite all the advantages just summarized, only 38 percent of US high schools and 14 percent of middle schools teach all nineteen sexual health topics considered essential by the Centers for Disease Control (Blanton 2019).

It is important to understand this landscape because this is where many of our journeys about sex begin. Through my interviews, I was able to zoom in to the specific stories that help bring to life the experiences people have had in all types of sex education including those listed above. After months of asking strangers and friends about their experiences learning about sex, it began to feel like a science, no––a three-step program that reinforces sex as a taboo, deviant topic. The steps are as follows:

1. Shame in the household
The first step in this "program" starts at home where there can be shame and embarrassment around anything related to sex. Asking about anything remotely sex related could result in punishment or reprimanding.

I remember the first time I heard the word "sex." My family and I were living in a yellow house in a quiet neighborhood in South Georgia and *Two and a Half Men* was playing loudly in my parents' room. I was so intrigued. Charlie Sheen had blithely said the word *"sex,"* and the audience immediately exploded into laughter and applause. As a seven-year-old, I was confused. *What did I miss? What was the punch line?* My mind could not even fathom that a single word could elicit such a response. When I broached the question to my parents, I was reprimanded for being, as they told me, "corrupt." This was the first time I heard either of those words.[1]

It is normal for young people and kids to ask about these things. It shows their curiosity. Too often, adults and parents react negatively to that curiosity, projecting shame and disgust.

Shame and disgust around sex are learned responses.

On my writing journey, I encountered many resources that help guide parents and adults in conversations about sex, for themselves and the young people in their lives. You can peek at these resources located in the back of the book.

The truth is that sex seeps into everyone's life. It does not matter if you are seventy, twenty something, or a teenager. Everyone has a story about how they learned or didn't learn about sex, and at some point, along the way, we were hushed, punished, or made to feel embarrassed for wanting to know more.

2. **Research on Incognito mode**
The second step in the program comes in the form of independent research: the late-night Googling (i.e., "sex" "girls kissing" "what is oral sex" "blue waffles"), explanations during recess, swapping bits of misinformation with friends

---

1   I spent a great deal of my childhood associating and conflating the word "sex" with "corrupt."

and peers, rumors around school about who did what, where, and with whom. Most kids are uninhibited in their questions. Only later, when we receive social cues to do so, do we learn to fake understanding or feign disinterest in the things we do not know about. Many adults have perfected this skill. Especially when it comes to sensitive topics like sex, it's easier to pretend like you know it all than to reveal that some of your questions remain unanswered.

Judgment is a close companion here. We judge ourselves, and as a result, we judge others.

3. Sex education at school

And finally, cue Vinh's experience: some version of a barely there sex education that sets cis, straight sex (also known as PVI, penis vagina intercourse) as the norm. Boys in this room, girls in that room.[2] A crash course on menstruation and pregnancy for the girls. A thorough description of STIs for everyone else. If you're lucky, maybe the condom and banana trope found time to shine. Pleasure is an afterthought and, if mentioned, is linked only to male pleasure. Queer, trans, and gender nonconforming identities are nonexistent. Topics like race and gender exist in a separate dimension.

In this book, there are no divisions or parts for just boys or just girls. Gender is more expansive than this. In this book, sex is defined as any meaningful experience of pleasure, not simply penis/vagina intercourse. In this book, pleasure is not a luxury. It is a human right.

---

2   Dividing kids by gender when they are learning about sex for the first time solidifies the gender binary in its full rigidity at a critical point in a kid's sexual journey.

The term sex positivity was invented to combat a lot of the things I've mentioned. It was intended to take a flashlight and shine a light on everything that gets missed when this three-step program is our primary way of learning about sex.

"IS NOTHING SACRED?"

I was an impressionable eighteen-year-old when I moved across the country from my small town in South Georgia to attend Stanford University in California. On campus, I was introduced to the term "sex positive." It was on a sticker outside of a Residential Assistant's dorm room. In glittery bright colors, it defined sex positivity as enthusiastic support of an individual's decision to have or not have sex.

My personal three-step program on sex education had not included "sex positivity" and immediately I felt uneasy. The idea of talking openly about sex made me recoil. I remember thinking: "Is nothing sacred?" in response to such an unabashed declaration about sex. From then on, whenever I was confronted with messaging or conversations that I thought would be better kept more private, I would go back to that idea of sanctity. I am not ready to talk about it yet, but a lot of this was informed by growing up in the Catholic Church. Maybe in my next book.

In retrospect, my response to the mention of sex came from a need to protect myself. When people spoke openly about things that I was told to be silent about, it triggered a reaction in me. It still does. I think it is only human to feel taken aback when conversations materialize around topics that you'd only ever thought about in your head.

The sex positivity sticker was explicit about supporting people's decision to not have sex. Despite this, I still felt that familiar pang that comes when you feel alone or weird. I remember thinking, *this sticker is not for me.* I, Mo Asebiomo, did not possess the highlighter, glittery attitude about sex, and I couldn't put my finger on why. Maybe because I hadn't seen people who looked like me talk openly about sex? Maybe because I wasn't sexually active and had no plans of being so? Maybe the answer was in the mixture of shame and self-righteousness I felt in my decision to not have sex. Maybe it dated back to when I was seven and I was called "corrupt" for asking what sex was.

THE MYTHS ABOUT SEX

A few months after seeing that sticker for the first time, a friend of mine confidently told me that I was not, in fact, sex positive. This was in response to the fact that I had chosen at the time not to have sex. Ah yes, one of the biggest prevailing myths of sex positivity: you do NOT, in fact, need to be having sex or even want to have sex to be a sex positive person. Despite this, many people still believe that, as well as some of the other things listed here:

- You must be having sex to be sex positive.
- If you are not having sex with someone, you cannot access pleasure.
- You cannot explore your sexuality without having sexual encounters or sexual partners.
- People who do not identify as queer cannot explore their sexuality.
- Sex-ed should just be about sexual intercourse.
- Sex is just about sexual intercourse.

- Sex involves only a penis and vagina.
- Pleasure is a luxury.
- Sex should be a private matter.
- If parents talk to their kids about sex, their kids will have sex.
- Sharing your sex stories is necessary to be sex positive.
- People who are curious about sex are perverted.

Do you believe or were you taught any of these things?

To be honest, it was easy coming up with that list because I definitely believed them all at one point. And I am still unlearning them.

This book starts by debunking the myths mentioned above while also fleshing them out more so we can see their connections to systems like racism, homophobia, transphobia, white settler colonialism, capitalism, and more. If this is beginning to sound political, good! Sex is and continues to be political.

I look back now and have a better understanding of what the sparkly Sex Positive sticker was trying to promote. Once I could start seeing through my own shame, I began to recognize the common pitfall of conflating sex-positivity with being "pro-sex." This explains why so many people think you must be having sex or have had sex to be sex positive.

When sex positivity is reduced to celebrating people's decisions to have or not have sex, a lot of important information is missed. We miss how sex positivity isn't merely a trend but a framework that seeks to inform, heal, and reveal while addressing rampant social oppressions in our society. We miss the opportunity to apply a pleasure and consent-based approach to all parts of our life.

In my writing I wondered, *What questions can we begin to ask ourselves and others in order to unearth and reclaim the political origins of sex positivity?*

This is what I've got so far:

- How can we trace the myths and misinformation of sex positivity back to forces of the patriarchy, white settler colonialism and anti-Blackness in the United States?
- What would it look like to approach sex positivity from a Black feminist lens?
- What can we learn from Pleasure Activism, disability justice, our past and contemporary trans leaders and figures? What can we unlearn from the shame that often accompanies our first lessons of sex?
- How can we nuance the conversation? Muddle the black and white and learn to dance in the gray in-between?

Just so we're all on the same page, however, I will let you know what this book is and is not.

THIS BOOK IS NOT
–An expert breakdown of sexual health, including STI education and protective sex.

–A beginner's guide to understanding the spectrum of gender, sexuality, gender expression, and sex assigned at birth.

–A guide on sex positions and how to have the best orgasms of your life (though I do wish many orgasms for your future!).

–A memoir of my own sexual history and what I learned along the way.

THIS BOOK IS
–Broadly questioning how systems of power and oppression have dictated the way we view and understand sex.

–Exploring and considering themes like pleasure, racism, ableism, fatphobia, and anti-Blackness in their proximity to sex education.

–Utilizing a Black feminist lens (me!) to examine the short-falls of the majority of the United States public sex education (or lack thereof).

I'll let you in on a little secret.

When my friend, years ago, told me I was not sex positive, I was actually relieved. A part of me was glad to finally hear someone confirm what I had secretly feared and believed to be true for most of my life: I, a dark-skinned Black woman could not exist as a sexual being.

I had carried that "truth" for as long as I could remember, dating back to middle school when I told myself it was a "superpower" that none of the white boys in my class would ever consider me as a romantic equal. In my mind, I was untouchable! Now as an adult, I have the language to understand how dehumanizing it is to have parts of yourself be made small. I am sure I am not the only one who has felt this way. Thus, an intention of mine is to center and acknowledge the communities too often left behind in conversations about sex and pleasure. Dominant narratives and tropes from the Western canon have no space in my writing journey.

And as I began to piece together the parts of this book, I realized more and more that we are all not as alone we think we are. Somewhere along the way, we were made to feel as though we were the only people in the whole world to think these things, to wonder, question or imagine.

While writing this book, I spent time digging through comment sections, reading twitter threads, and on chats of workshops and webinars. I was doing my best to keep "an ear to the ground." I wanted to hear from real people about their real experiences. Many of my interviews with sexuality educators, psychologists, sex workers, sexual health advocates and social justice organizers, even professors, started with a direct message on Instagram.

This was an intentional pushback to the way academia prides itself on being the source of empirical knowledge. I spoke with experts in the field of sexuality studies whose primary platform to reach their audience were podcasts, social media accounts, and digital publications. I learned a lot from them, and I learned a lot from myself as well. Hopefully, this book will be the impetus to your continued learning.

In truth, this book is a letter to my queer siblings, radical thinkers, questioning millennials, and soulful Gen-Zers.

This is for the instructors and educators in Gender, Sexuality & Feminist studies who need a fresh, updated perspective about the academic landscape they have spent years getting acclimated to. This is for the Black and brown sexologists who have contributed so much to this work and are looking to see their values and missions reflected back to them. This is for the Black, queer, and trans kids out there. This is for you.

Phew! And we're just getting started! Keep reading and come along on my journey of decolonizing sex positivity. Hopefully, I will challenge some of your ideas, validate your experiences and most importantly, make you feel less alone.

BREAKING DOWN
THE BUZZWORDS

———

Among all the shifts this year, phrases like
"decolonize" "liberate" "dismantle" and "abolish"
have become popularized with reminders
of what we're up against and what we can
do to envision and enact a way forward.

I'll say over and over again. It is okay if
these concepts feel overwhelming! But it
should never stop us from practicing.

—JEZZ CHUNG

For most of my life in academia, sharing knowledge and "demonstrating my intelligence" was reduced to the skill of throwing big words around in a grammatically sound way. I spent most of my time in college sitting in discussion groups and writing essays about things I barely had a firm grasp on. It is an elitist skill I might add, to navigate academia by saying a bunch of nothing. Especially as a kid who grew up reading SAT vocabulary books, I still have to catch myself when saying a bunch of nothing. When we talk about sex (especially in a context of decolonization and anti-racism) it is easy to use a lot of language that ends up not saying much.

"Healing," "empowerment," "radical," and "decolonize" name a few of the buzzwords I have encountered. To be frank, I absolutely love these words. When I read and say these words, I feel powerful! Language can do that. Think back to a time when you encountered a word or phrase that perfectly captured your experience. It felt good, didn't it? When we can tell our stories with language that is carefully crafted for us, it feels amazing. That act, in and of itself, *is* a taste of liberation. And so, language can be our first tool for empowering ourselves and creating a liberated lifestyle.

We must also be mindful of how we use language intended to help us. It can be easy to throw around words and phrases without truly doing the work of understanding what they mean and symbolize. A reminder: it is less about the words we are using and more about the ideas and messages we are conveying. In this book, I have tried to get into the practice of saying things quite plainly and simply.

So here, I have set aside a glossary of terms related to social oppression to introduce the big ideas I throw out in the book. Social oppression is something that happens between categories of people. This is not the same as the oppressive behavior of individuals.

When individuals *behave* in oppressive ways, we would refer to it as discrimination. Bias and prejudice describe the oppressive *beliefs* held by that individual. In cases of social oppression, all members of the dominant and subordinate groups are involved, regardless of individual attitudes or behavior (Crossman 2019). These types of social oppression, while existing in larger systems, can still be exemplified in the behavior of individuals.

I start with the most significant types of social oppression as they relate to topics of sex and sexuality. I include a definition and questions to get your mind thinking. As you will see throughout the book, these questions guide my writing and research.

Keep in mind that the following all exist on a spectrum (meaning there is a range of experiences a person has within each example of social oppression) and bear in mind that they all interact with one another and exacerbate the effects on society.

ANTI-BLACKNESS
Anti-Blackness in the United States refers to prejudice and oppressive treatment toward Black people and Black culture. Anti-Blackness is not only encouraged, it is rewarded. When it comes to sex, some questions I think about are:

Who is deserving of pleasure?
- How do our beliefs and opinions change when we think about Black people and sex versus white people? For one group, perhaps sex is seen as dirty, immoral or an

undeserved luxury while for the other group, sex is normalized and considered a healthy part of life. The perceptions and reactions we have about sex do not live in a vacuum. Because we live in a world where most societies, if not all, are anti-Black, we must confront how stereotypes and negative views on Black people seep into our internalized perspective of sex in the Black community.

How do systems that "police" the Black body inform traditional sex education and attitudes toward sex?

- *Policing* in this context refers to the implicit and explicit ways our laws and social norms control bodily expression and appearance, namely of Black people. A good place to start is to reflect on how we socialize girls and women. Many of us were taught, as young girls, to sit with our legs closed, have good posture, and aim for graceful and delicate movements. This as an example of female and women bodies being "policed." Body policing in the Black community takes on a particular tone because what is seen as the "norm" or "appropriate" is typically anti-Black. In later chapters, I will discuss considering how sex education comes from schools and institutions that also seek to police Black people.

Throughout the book, I refer to the Black community and Black scholars. Know that the connections I make do not just pertain to the Black experience. When we begin to assess and understand the lives of Black people as one of the most oppressed groups in the United States, it gives us the opportunity to hold a mirror to ourselves to understand the ways in which others have been subject to similar harm and abuses.

We can learn the ways our experiences are shockingly similar or vastly different.

WHITE SUPREMACY CULTURE

White supremacy culture translates to a continued elevation of the value(s) of white people and the western world. As a result, it perpetuates whiteness as the desired standard and norm. Consequently, when we learn about sex in the United States, it should be assumed that the entire premise of sex is informed by whiteness. Who wrote the sex-ed books and material you're reading? The images depicted in such materials—were they portrayed primarily by white, skinny, able-bodied people? If porn was your first exposure to sex, did you see white bodies?

White supremacy is built on the tenets of colonialism. The late Patrick Wolfe, scholar, and author of "Settler Colonialism and the Elimination of the Native," writes extensively of how invasion (or settler colonialism) is a structure not a singular event (Wolfe 2006). Essentially, what this means is that white settler colonialism is a way of being that penetrates the cultural membrane of a society.

Kenneth Jones and Tema Okun would agree with me, stating, "Culture is powerful precisely because it is so present and at the same time so very difficult to name or identify." In their workbook "From Dismantling Racism: A Workbook for Social Change Groups," Jones and Okun deliberately outline the characteristics of white supremacy culture, which show up in organizations. These characteristics include but are not limited to perfectionism, a sense of urgency, defensiveness, quantity over quality, worship of the written word, paternalism, either/or thinking, power hoarding and objectivity (Jones & Okun 2001).

My writing relies and builds upon the definitions and understanding of white supremacy culture as outlined by Kenneth Jones and Tema Okun in their workbook and Patrick Wolfe's writing in his acclaimed paper.

How do these white supremacy characteristics tie into the way we learn and understand sex and sexuality? What does sex negativity look like in a culture founded on exploitation, control, and domination?

CAPITALISM, GRIND CULTURE & THE LAZINESS LIE

Capitalism exists in an economic structure driven by competition and scarcity where inequality is justified.

In the words of Tricia Hersey, founder of the Nap Ministry, grind culture is white supremacy and capitalism blended together. "It's the thing that started when our ancestors were on plantations—the culture of seeing human beings as machines. The word 'grind'—when you think about gears and grinding on a machine—it sees our bodies and who we are as just being machines for production. That's the center of the foundation of the belief, and everything about rest has been distorted because of that (Cullors 2020)."

While the origin of the sentiment of grind culture dates back to slavery, we see it every day in the over-emphasis of being productive at all times. It shows up in our daily behaviors and habits where a sense of urgency is always present. It shows up when we deny our bodies rest and comfort for the sake of productivity. It shows up in the way that burnout and exhaustion from work are status symbols or markers of success. It shows up in how we characterize any behavior that deviates from productivity as laziness.

The laziness lie teaches us that our productivity determines our worth and focusing on anything other than outcomes means we aren't working hard enough (Price 2021). Everything we do can quickly become about success or failure, including sex and pleasure.

How do capitalist ideologies and tendencies inform "good sex" or being sex positive?

ABLE-ISM

Capitalism, grind culture, and the laziness lie are all the older cousins of able-ism. Ableism is a byproduct of capitalism in which the inherent worth of human beings are tied to their physical or mental ability. Conor Arpwell, a self-declared socialist and trade unionist, tweets, "Unlearning ableism requires a fundamentally anti-capitalist change in perspective. Specifically, it necessitates that you believe in the inherent worth of human beings, regardless of someone's social position or productive potential."

What are some of the inherently ableist ideas embedded in sex positivity? How can disability justice elevate our conversations of sex positivity?

TRANSPHOBIA & TRANSMISOGYNY

Outside of being discrimination, hostility, and/or violence toward transgender people, transphobia specifically reinforces the gender binary instead of gender as a spectrum. Similar to anti-Blackness, transphobia is weaved into the fabric of our society.[3]

How have transphobic principles of traditional sex education remained intact in progressive sex-positive movements? In what ways do myths of sex positivity directly harm and target trans individuals and genderqueer communities?

MISOGYNOIR

Misogynoir refers to the dual discrimination that Black women face for their gender and racial identity.

How have white women become the face of the sex positivity movement, and how does their presence define the consequential norms and attitudes about it? How has misogyny, specifically misogynoir, enabled the perpetuation of dangerous and false messaging around sex positivity?

AGEISM

For these purposes, ageism reflects how older generations are stripped of their sexuality as they age. This happens as a result of a society and culture whose infrastructure and ideologies do not center on elders. Additionally, ageism emerges when we diminish the agency and bodily autonomy of children.

---

3   Transphobia is also a sin.

What are the consequences of not talking about sex for older people? How do we dehumanize the older generation in regard to their sexual identities? How is this an extension of the idea of who is deserving of pleasure?

FATPHOBIA

Fatphobia is responsible for the standard of equating beauty and good health to body size. In the words of Sonya Renee Taylor, "There is no standard of health that is achievable for all bodies. Our belief that there should be anchors the systematic oppression of ableism and reinforces the notion that people with illnesses and disabilities have defective bodies rather than different bodies (Taylor 2018)."

Who have we continually excluded from the sex-positive movement? How does that mirror society's standard for who is allowed to be sexual? How does fatphobia STILL show up in the sex positivity movement?

What can be learned as we work toward a decolonized framework to understand sex, bodies, privilege, and power? How can we begin to center liberation over "acceptance?"

WEAPONS AGAINST THE SYSTEM

Thanks to a long legacy of writers, activists, organizers, poets, artists, and others who created tools to reimagine realities and make the revolution irresistible, there are weapons against the aforementioned systems and practices. Disability justice, Black feminism, queer theory, and Indigenous knowledge are a short list of "antidotes" to heal and collectively grow.[4]

A point of feedback from my editors was the number of broad claims I made without sufficient evidence. I point largely to capitalism and white supremacy as the culprits of why we live in a deeply sex negative society, but my claims are "unfounded." Where's the proof?

The proof is inside you.

I think of the words of Andrea Ranae, "Everything you wish to dismantle resides within you too."

I am writing about what I have found that resides within me. I use words like "recognize," "unlearn," "appreciate," and "cultivate a deep understanding," in all my chapters. This is all just an invitation to think about how the things I write about resides within you too.

I am aware of the desire to learn things quickly. We want things in a formula, a webinar, a crash course, or a how-to guide. But when it comes to deep learning and unlearning, there are no quick answers. In the words of the impressive movement and platform, The Nap Ministry, "There are no quick tips to deprogramming from grind culture and crafting a rest practice in a capitalist world. Maybe that's part of the problem. We want 'quick,' magic bullets all the time."

---

4   I would suggest looking up care work, femme emotional labor, access and crip skills specifically.

So, as you read this book, take breaks. Take naps. Come back to it when you can. When you feel a tightness in your chest, breathe. When you inwardly cringe, at a memory, idea, or anything your unconscious mind resurfaces, pause.

My scope is far reaching, so I ask for your grace when I miss or forget to acknowledge nuances, exceptions, and pitfalls. At the end of the book, I've included some questions to consider and sit with. If I do it right, you should answer them with more questions.

You may notice that throughout the book, I will not define sex as one thing or one act. These things are up to *you* to decide. I am here to offer a framework, insight, language and a friendly voice to tell you that you are not alone.

We must work to decolonize all facets of our life. For now, I hope we can get the conversation started with sex positivity.

SEX POSITIVITY AND WHY IT NEEDS TO BE DECOLONIZED

———

Why does it feel like every history lesson begins with a random white, usually European man coining a term?[5]

In this context, I wonder how many Indigenous people and communities of color were practicing what we now understand to be "sex positivity" before Wilhelm Reich, an Austrian doctor and psychoanalyst, showed up in the 1920s to coin the phrase. I refer to this as "whitewashing."

Whitewashing refers to when a culture's traditions and histories are changed to satisfy Western stereotypes. I recently saw a phrase on social media that described whitewashing history as creating "white American historical fan fiction." It made me laugh because it was true. Understanding

———

5   Even the concept of "coining a term" is colonial. Colonialist values
     emphasize written language as the centerpiece of knowledge.

whitewashing and why it happens is the first step to decolonizing sex positivity.

My intention throughout the entire writing of the book is to *strip* the sex positive movement from its proclaimed white American origins and reclaim it for marginalized communities. In Alex Intaffi's editorial, "White Privilege in Sex and Relationship Therapy," they recognize how much of sexuality literature is rooted in a White or Western perspective (Intaffi 2012). Radicalizing or "decolonizing" is the antithesis of whitewashing. To put it plainly, operating from a decolonial perspective seeks to reclaim the history that has been taken while honoring what we still have. I borrow these words from Tina Curiel-Allen, a queer Xicana/Boricua writer and activist.

Meenadchi, author of *Decolonizing Non-Violent Communication,* frames the practice of decolonizing as a gentle and consistent practice of interrogation: "Who put this thought there? Where did I learn this truth?"

DEFINING SEX POSITIVITY

Let's start with the reality that sex positivity is not always positive. In fact, the foundation of sex positivity acknowledges that people have all sorts of relationships with sex. "The truth is that sex can be painful, regrettable, traumatizing, and forgettable," says Miri Mogilevsky in their article "10 Things Sex Positivity Is Not."

The sex positive movement acknowledges this and builds on that understanding. To be sex positive means that you (yes, you!) not only respect the many orientations, backgrounds and experiences that exist and are different from your own, but you also strive to learn about the systems and ideologies that could inform them.

Mogilevsky writes:

> *I want a sex positivity movement that is here for all the trauma survivors, all the asexual and aromatic folks, all the people who don't love their bodies, everyone who's ever felt ambivalent about sex, anyone who feels like sex has done them more harm than good. I want a sex positivity that fights for these people, too (Mogilevsky 2016).*

Decolonizing sex positivity means updating our current understanding of sex positivity and the sexual revolution to be intersectional. When I say intersectional, I refer to the term in its purest form as coined by Kimberle Crenshaw. Intersectionality is more than simply holding a multitude of identities. Intersectionality is about the different ways that people experience privilege and wield power as a result of those identities. It is an examination of the overlap and nuance of prejudice and discrimination that gets mapped onto multi-layered identities.

Apryl Alexander seconds this in her research published in the 2019 *Journal of Black Sexuality & Relationships.* In her article "Sex for All," Alexander writes, "Ultimately, sex positivity should center on the experiences (i.e., recognizing one's position of power and privilege and shifting to anti-oppressive tactics) of marginalized communities and normalize the range of fluid sexual experiences."

When I use the words "sex positivity," I think of it as a grown-up version of sex education. In college, I was exposed to sex positivity as a framework for adults to continue their learning and unlearning about sex and sexual identities. Writing this book has taken me a step further to discover the radical potential of sex positivity. Especially as predominantly white, straight, and cis-gendered women have occupied the sex education space, it has been a consequence that their voices have been amplified over others resulting in public ignorance over how sex positivity can be informed by decolonial praxis and anti-racist perspectives. Author and thought leader, Adrienne Maree Brown refers to that as "pleasure activism."[6] Brown is a direct testimony to the rise of Black femme, gender non-binary, and women of color writing their realities into existence.

Many of the false messaging around sex positivity is by no means accidental. It is calculated. It is precise. And obviously, it is harmful. It is especially harmful to women of color and Black women/femme who are policed in their sexuality and are offered a whitewashed movement as the only tool for liberation.

We know that the tools for our liberation will not come from the systems that oppress us. Cue Audre Lorde's famous essay, "The master's tools will never dismantle the master's house." In the same vein, the whitewashed history and movement of sex positivity will not bring us closer to freedom and wholeness. In fact, it will only further reinforce a certain

---

6   I understand pleasure activism as a synonym for decolonizing sex positivity.

type of dehumanization but will do so with glittery words and pretty sayings. "Love your body!" "Sex is empowerment." "Find healing through masturbation."

While some of these messages have the right intention, they are often shared in an environment that does little to acknowledge the complex histories of shame that continue to be reinforced by culture and society. Very few of us have easy and simple relationships with our own sexuality, let alone with the sexual experiences we have had. Many of us have been inspired to cultivate a sex-positive culture specifically because of some of those complicated feelings and histories.

In the words of Nafessa Dawoodbhow, "What are ways that people with intersecting identities, especially people of color, can stay true to their whole selves and honor the complexities of all their identities?"

As part of answering that question, I explored the online landscape that has been a platform for people of color to begin reclaiming their rightful spot in sex education. In her article, "Sex for All," Alexander explains that, "Due to stigmatization, sex-positive communities tend to flourish online, which could be further enabled by improved reach and lack of geographical barriers, as well as increased real and perceived anonymity for participants (Alexander 2019)." Instagram, specifically, has become a popular tool for bridging the gaps in our sex education and making space for the sex-ed we've always deserved but never received. One note of caution, we must be vigilant and intentional about the content we consume. For many, this is the first real exposure to what sex-ed could have and should have looked like.

With this in mind, it is paramount to know the backgrounds and intentions of the people behind social media accounts to control for information that is merely trendy and potentially incorrect.

Despite the growing popularity of sex-positive values, dominant US attitudes remain sex-negative with barriers still existing for Black and non-Black people of color to access the sexuality space. Cameron Glover, a Black femme writer and sex educator says, "In fact, the field still largely remains whitewashed, with white sexuality professionals holding and often gatekeeping the majority of visibility, support, and public clout. Despite the contributions that Black sexuality professionals, in particular, have made to the field spanning decades, we are still largely underrepresented and under supported compared to white sexuality professionals. And though change is happening, that change is slow."

DECOLONIZING WHILE BLACK
It is important to acknowledge and establish both the positionality of the voices in this discussion as well as my own positionality as the curator. In a space where the white gaze dominates the canon, I want to be transparent about what context this book provides and what contexts are missing.

Although I do hold the identity of a Black woman in the United States, I want to distinguish my experience as a first-generation child of Nigerian immigrants who voluntarily migrated to the US for economic reasons, not a Black American whose diasporic narrative descends from forced slavery. As a Black woman, the voice of Black feminist scholars resonates with my world view and guides my writing. I think it is powerful when we synthesize Black feminist perspectives with Native or Indigenous decolonialist frameworks and I have tried to do that justice in my writing. I acknowledge that while my book does explore the tenets of sex positivity as they relate to ongoing colonialist values and cultures, it fails to rely heavily on North American Indigenous scholars and practitioners. Rather, my sources come from a diverse array of backgrounds, principally people of color in academia and sexuality education with the majority being Black.

I ask for grace in my writing and acknowledge the work I and others must do to center Indigenous land, Indigenous sovereignty, and Indigenous ways of thinking when claiming to decolonize.

The catalyst for me exploring the decolonization discussion was to confront these complex and intimidating issues with fervor to reclaim, dismantle, and ultimately abolish the systems of oppression that stand before us. My hope is that I am not the last queer Black woman writing about sex positivity in this way. I do not think I will be.

Finally, I use the term decolonizing with the acknowledgment of Native Indigenous land sovereignty and our presence on un-ceded, stolen land as inheritors of settler colonialism.

SEX SOCIALIZATION AS A VEHICLE FOR SOCIAL CHANGE

———

Decolonizing sex positivity means recognizing the degree to which sex positivity or sexual liberation is tied to collective liberation. In order to appreciate that connection, we need to unlearn that sex is merely what happens between the sheets.

It means recognizing that sex education's focus on the biology of sex and subsequent centering of STIs is done in contrast to intentional sex socialization.[7]

With this type of education in schools, "liability frameworks" and "objective science" become the biggest actors, and anti-Blackness and transphobia (as seen throughout the origin and history of the United States) are cleverly hidden, critical ingredients.

———

7   Sex socialization refers to the multidimensional process by which knowledge, attitudes, and values about sexuality are acquired.

Sex education that socializes our sexual identities in positive and healthy ways can be a powerful vehicle for social change. Activating that social change begins with advocating for the rights of all people to accurate information, comprehensive sexuality education and the full spectrum of sexual and reproductive health services (Sexual Information and Education Council of the United States 2021).

THE MOST FUNDAMENTAL MYTH WE NEED TO DEBUNK IS THAT SEX IS ONLY ABOUT SEXUAL INTERCOURSE.
Believing this myth is a distraction. Lorde says it herself in the opening lines of "Uses of the Erotic."

"In order to perpetrate itself, every oppression must corrupt or distort those various sources of power within the culture of the oppressed that can provide energy for change (Lorde 2016)."

Lorde continues in one of my favorite excerpts:
This is one reason why the erotic is so feared, and so often relegated to the bedroom alone, when it is recognized at all. For once we begin to feel deeply all the aspects of our lives, we begin to demand from ourselves and from our life-pursuits that they feel in accordance with that joy which we know ourselves to be capable of (Lorde 2016).

When I imagine positive sex socialization in schools, I think of reading work by the likes of Audre Lorde and helping people develop an identity and thoughtfulness of who they are and what it means for them to feel deeply in their lives.[8]

Instead, my experience of sex education was minimized to a specific subset of sexual health education that overly emphasized sexually transmitted infections. In the words of Dr. Eric Spankle, the Associate Professor of Clinical Psychology and Sexuality Studies at Minnesota State University, focusing only on STIs is like going to culinary school and only learning about food poisoning.

This type of education perpetuates the stigma attached to STIs and furthers the spread of misinformation. I remember being shown graphic images of STIs in sex-ed classes just to learn that the majority of common STIs are in fact asymptotic.

Emily L. Depasse is a writer and researcher redefining the narratives around STIs and relationships. Depasse is also the founder of SexELDucation, a platform that serves as an invaluable resource and all-encompassing space for those seeking more comprehensive approaches to confronting stigma.

Emily says the following:
We're taught "avoid avoid avoid" until one day, we can no longer fly by the seat of invincibility. Those diagnosed with an STI like herpes often do a deep dive into research following the diagnosis. They learn about

---

8   I would suggest reading Lorde's work and examining her definition of the "erotic" and understanding the parellels it has to the notion of sex socialization.

antivirals, disclosure, transmission, and effective com-munication strategies with partners. When disclosing to potential partners, it's not just the "I have an STI" part of the conversation that's difficult. It's the confron-tation of someone who likely has never been taught to have these conversations, or that these conversations even exist. Or most often, that they'd find themselves in this position.

Ironically, the same labor that many who live with STIs do to understand their diagnosis is merely the baseline of what should be the public level of knowledge. Instead, the rubric of the majority of sex education in the US relies on science as objective truth and frameworks in liability reduction.

LIABILITY REDUCTION IN SEX EDUCATION
Liability frameworks, risk management, and capitalism are among the biggest players when it comes to our "education" around sex.

Julie Fukunaga, a dear friend of mine would agree. Fukunaga says, "I think so much of sex-ed is about crisis management. Liability is all it is. It's like, okay if we teach abstinence, kids won't have kids at sixteen, and then we won't have pregnant sixteen-year-olds. If we teach abstinence, girls will learn how to say no, and then boys won't coerce them into having sex until they're ready. We'll teach you the bare minimum like condoms, so you won't get STDs."

Fukunaga's assertions are confirmed in Grace Totter's 2018 Harvard Graduate School of Education article titled "Sex

Education that Goes beyond Sex." Historically, the measure of a good sex education program has been in the numbers: marked decreases in the rates of sexually transmitted diseases, teen pregnancies, and pregnancy-related drop-outs (Totter, 2018)." And why does a legalistic, liability approach feel all too familiar? It's because capitalism sets up an environment in which accountability is singular and crisis management is normalized. The only way we've been taught to create systems from scratch begins with a sense of liability. As a result, we uplift independence, agency and self-sufficiency while shunning interdependent, collaboration and reliance—all key ingredients for healthy sex socialization.

SCIENCE AS AN OBJECTIVE IN SEX EDUCATION

Western colonial beliefs use science as a means of control. People see science as an objective when in reality, science still exists in a social domain. (*social domain* in the sense that it is not impervious to societal beliefs and interpretations.) Once upon a time not long ago, eugenics were grounded in science. Things like systemic racism, prejudice, and homophobia continue to be grounded in science. In this way, scientific knowledge is not fixed, "It shifts as cultural prejudice is revealed and challenged (Menon 2020)." Nevertheless, science tends to have a lot of credibility, which is why it is so easy to use it as a political tool.

When sex is reduced to a "biological action" happening in a vacuum for the sake of science, there is no opportunity to talk about the spectrum of relevant themes like power or equally as important, pleasure. Alok Menon, author of *Beyond the Gender Binary*, would agree in their own words saying that "science is used as a rhetorical strategy for a normative goal (Menon 2020)." Essentially, it's not about science. It's about power.

Going back to Vinh's comparison of his sex education being similar to learning about photosynthesis, he adds yet another comparison. He says, "They might as well have been talking about pigs having sex—any lesson delivered was devoid of any semblance of the accompanying sociocultural context." What do pigs having sex and photosynthesis have in common? They can both be distilled to scientific, biological acts.

In Vinh's eyes, it is basically a cop out. Vinh says that if schools can get away with just defining sex, they don't actually have to teach anything useful. If educators are not teaching you how to safely engage in sex, how to protect yourself, the ideas of consent, (all aspects of sex socialization) they are not liable; things like sexual assault happens, or pregnancies occur. In other words, teaching about sex in a scientific framework allows it to be socially disconnected, and by doing so absolves schools of the responsibility.

This logic also justifies the omission of teachings around all forms of queerness. Because if having sex with someone from the same sexual group is deemed to have no productive function and thereby is not considered scientifically significant, there is really no need to talk about queerness.

Vinh wonderfully puts in plain words what scholar, Chad Mosher writes in their widely acclaimed article submitted to *The Counseling Psychologist* in May 2017 titled, "Historical

Perspectives of Sex Positivity: Contributing to a New Paradigm within Counseling Psychology."

He writes,

> *Sex negative paradigms reduce sex to a series of behavioral skills and functions centered on reproduction, and restrict sexual expression to compulsory heterosexuality, monogamy, and an active man in pursuit of a passive woman. Fluid sexual expressions, experiences of sexual minorities and/or queer individuals, non-monogamous relationships, people of color, older adults, and asexual individuals are marginalized, pathologized, and criminalized when cast against a template of heteronormativity (Mosher 2017).*

Centering sex as a purely biological function is not only incredibly reductive and out of touch, it is harmful. It robs people and communities of information that will impact their lives whether they're having sex or not.

In one of their interviews, George M. Johnson, author of *All Boys Aren't Blue* references the saying, "When white folks catch a cold, Black folks get pneumonia" in regard to misinformation and silence around sex in the Black community.

In other words, harmful messaging around sex may pose hardships for some white kids, but the room for error can be deadly for Black kids. I will add on to that and include not just Black kids, but most children of color, especially those who are queer, gender nonconforming, trans, and/or disabled.

Johnson is a prominent journalist and LGBTQIA+ activist. Their book, *All Boys Aren't Blue* is a series of personal essays that explore their adolescence and college years as a Black, queer boy in New Jersey and Virginia. Johnson continues, "I have a serious disdain for how Black kids have to go through trial and error for everything, and simply because we just won't talk about it, or we won't put it out there or we feel like they're too young to discuss it [sex]. And it's like again, they're discussing it. Whether you're around when they're discussing it or giving them the resources to discuss it, they're still going to discuss it (Johnson 2020)."

The research of Dr. Tracie Gilbert, a sexuality educator, researcher and founder of *The Sex-Ed of Black Folks* podcast (TSOB), confirms Johnson's words. In our interview, Dr. Gilbert shared the following:

> *When you look at the history of sex-ed especially through a public health lens, so much of it was built on the idea of demonizing Black sexuality and working to prevent and stop Black people from being sexual. It [sex-education] reflects the idea of wanting to preserve everyone's safety but what that really means and ends up looking like is we want Black people to keep their legs closed. No one explicitly says that but that's how it ends up getting doled out (Gilbert 2020).*

Dr. Gilbert's work mirrors the research of how anti-Blackness is woven into the history of sex education in the United States. The research of Courtney Q. Shah in their 2017 work, "Race, Gender, and Sex Education in Twentieth-Century America," delves into how reformers and educators often conveyed different messages and used different materials depending on the race of their students (Shah 2017). "Parents and administrators considered sexuality education even more dangerous in the context of a racially integrated classroom. The backlash against sex education in the schools kept pace with the backlash against integration, with each often used to bolster the other. Opponents of integration and sex education, for example, often used racial language to scare parents about what kids were learning and with whom (Shah 2017)."

From sex education to birth control and reproductive rights, the United States has a long, bleak history of anti-Blackness in shaping current systems, curriculums and laws around sex and sexuality.[9] The justification for such overt racism? Science, of course.

When we treat sex as mere biological information, it reinforces the history of science being used for power and control. As a result, sex education programs intentionally lack holistic initiatives around sex socialization making it an easy tool in service of the settler/colonial agenda.

---

9   I would recommend Dorothy E. Roberts's book, *Killing the Black Body* to start that conversation.

SILENCE AS THE TOOL OF THE OPPRESSOR

People have different relationships to sex and rightfully so. However, the United States is among many countries around the globe in which sex is a heavily stigmatized topic. For me, growing up, sex was taboo. At Stanford, it was quite the opposite. There were whole organizations and administrative positions all with the word "sex" in them. Suddenly what was formerly hidden was completely in open view.

Maybe you can relate to the experience of existing in two or more cultures that are incredibly different—even contradictory. This chapter is titled, "Silence as the tool of the oppressor" because when it comes to sex being taboo, it is more than just a "clash of cultures."

Decolonizing sex positivity means recognizing that silence has been and continues to be a tool of control in the hands of the oppressor. Cultures of silence benefit people in power and perpetrators of harm. Silence about things that matter will never be helpful. We see this within the code of silence in generations of domestic and sexual violence and abuse in families (Rakovec-Felser 2014). I think silence can be one of the strongest social forces that can be mobilized to protect and maintain abuse of power.

Here are the main consequences of not talking openly about sex:

- we signal that sex is bad and something to be ashamed of, which shows up in all kinds of ways, usually shame around our body and sexual desires
- we risk greater incidence of sexual trauma and sexually related health concerns

IT IS A MYTH THAT SEX SHOULD BE BEST KEPT AS A PRIVATE MATTER.

When we believe this myth, we feed into stigma, which survives off of silence.

Brianna Booth, the Director of Positive Sexuality at Stanford University says, "So often people think sex is uncomfortable to talk about and I'm like, no. What's uncomfortable is when things can't be talked about. For me, my discomfort comes from not being able to talk about things."

I agree with Brianna and have for a long time. My introduction to the concept came from the lens of race and identity. When I was doing research in my Psychology undergraduate program at Stanford, my focus was around young children's conceptions of race and identity. A common theme was the cocoon of silence that existed around conversations of race, especially for white families. Many educators and parents shy away from conversations about race in the hopes of creating "color-blind" kids or children who "don't see color." Color-blindness, while nice in theory, has no positive effect on institutional and structural racism. Instead, it creates white children who grow up to be white adults ignorant of the ways in which racism impacts people's lives.[10]

On top of that, these now white adults go on to experience a great deal of discomfort at the mention of race; they then have families and raise their own children and inadvertently perpetrate the same culture of silence. With my psychology background, I could not help but notice the parallels of the harmful consequences of breeding a culture of silence around sex.

An important aspect of my academic writing had to do with the malleable nature of the minds of young children. Throughout my academic career, I had countless conversations about neuroplasticity and how trauma impacts the brain and even language acquisition. Young children's brains are like sponges and cognitively speaking, early childhood has always been revered as a critical time of development. What do you think happens when adults silence children on conversations around sex, gender, and bodies at an early age? They conflate that stigma and the actual word to be one and the same—something bad. It's bad and that's why we do not talk about it. In psychology, we call this a *learned response,* and it is apparent in these examples.

Without sex education, kids learn through:

---

10 I would recommend Beverly Tatum's book, *Why Are All the Black Kids Sitting Together in the Cafeteria,* to start that conversation.

- online porn
- risky experimentation
- word on the street
- unsafe or abusive experiences

No one knows this better than Melissa Carnagey, the founder of Sex Positive Families. Sex Positive Families provides education and resources that help families raise sexually healthy children at every age and stage using a shame-free, comprehensive, and pleasure-positive approach. Melissa grew up in Texas where sex-education was abstinence-only. In fact, during our interview, they shared that they couldn't even recall a clear memory of being taught sex education—only some vague mentions of menstruation and having the class be divided into boys and girls. (Sound familiar?)

Growing up, sex was not talked about. Melissa says, "We learned to turn our heads and close our eyes while watching shows or comedy specials. There was never a discussion or conversation, so you were just left in the moment to act natural and pretend you were not aroused. I learned to act like I didn't care about whatever was happening on the screen."

Especially in the Black community there is a cost to the cocoons of silence we spin around ourselves. George M. Johnson emphasizes, "There's this belief if we keep it away from them, they won't do it. When realistically, keeping that type of information away from them doesn't stop them from doing it. It just means that more errors and mistakes get made along the way."

Carnagey would agree with Johnson. In Carnagey's years of working in the field as a social worker and sexuality educator for teens, they say, "The incidences of trauma that so many young people have are in sex-ed spaces. Sometimes, when trauma is talked about, the adults are talked about. The sad reality is that so many young people have sexual trauma and are coming into these education spaces as survivors and drivers of trauma."

Educators and adults who view sex-ed as nothing more than delivering "a bunch of biological information" risk teaching lessons that are triggering and can magnify existing trauma. Sex education should always be trauma informed.

RE-IMAGINING SEX EDUCATION: THE BIRDS & THE BEES

Puberty is an excellent way to begin conversations about sex, gender and our bodies. For many, puberty arrives at different times in people's lives. Often queer and trans people will have a "second puberty" in which their body changes in a way that aligns with their gender expression. A few days after interviewing Melissa Carnagey, I attended the workshop they led as part of Sex Positive Families: Growing into You! (Virtual) Puberty Workshop. Since the founding of Sex Positive Families in 2017, Melissa has serviced more than 821 families from over the world.

This specific workshop was a two-hour long program primarily for ten- to twelve-year-old kids. After just a few minutes of talking about puberty and sex with a bunch of adolescents and their parents, I was amazed. The openness and curiosity in which Melissa led the session was apparent from the very beginning when they opened with, "There are no wrong questions. There are no dirty questions."

Throughout the workshop, there were high-fives, lots of questions, and most importantly, everyone was learning. There were no breakout rooms for boys or for girls. Everyone learned about periods and masturbation and intersex people. We also talked about things like hormone blockers and the difference between someone's gender and the body they live in. My favorite question came from a kid who asked, "If you take a hormone blocker do you stay a kid forever?" and another, "Can you hold in your period like you hold in your pee?"

Melissa's workshop series is a prime example of what I mean when I talk of reimagining sex-education.

It looks like:
- Leading with curiosity rather than shame
- Using real and accurate terminologies for body parts and body processes
- For all kids to learn about all bodies, not just their own
- To include education around intersex people, which means imagery of intersex genitalia, just as we see illustrations of vaginas and penises
- Explaining what it means to be transgender and what hormone blockers are
- Framing puberty as more to do with what body parts we have and less about the gender we have
- Introducing the concept of consent at the first mention of sex

- Pictures of genitals/anatomy that are gender neutral (Sex Positive Families 2020)

What I saw in that workshop reignited all the reasons why I started writing this book. I could see with my own eyes how sex education could be a pathway for joy and liberation, even for twelve-year-olds.

ALL PARENTS ARE SEX EDUCATORS

At one point in the workshop, Melissa asks for a show of hands from the adults on the Zoom meeting to show how many of them talked about sex with their own parents. One lone hand was raised. Melissa took that moment to ask for empathy and patience from the kids. They said, "We didn't have anyone talk to us about these things, so please be patient with us. We [as parents] might feel awkward and a little uncomfortable talking to you about these things for the first time."

In this moment, I thought back to my memory of hearing the word "sex" for the first time and my parents' reaction. Adults project generations worth of trauma on young children when they begin to ask about sex because they were raised in a household that glorified a culture of silence. There are no bad players here—just grown-ups working through the same trauma they pass down to the young people in their lives.

Talking about sex, puberty, gender, sexuality and consent with a ten-year-old sounds pretty daunting. But it does not have to be this monumental occasion or talk. Young kids need mentors who offer ongoing support and validation as they age and mature. And the research shows that kids are receptive to this.

One of the prevailing reasons why parents and educators refrain from talking about sex is out of fear that a child will then go out and have sex. In the national surveys conducted by The National Campaign to Prevent Teen and Unplanned Pregnancy, teens report that their parents have the greatest influence over their decisions about sex—more than friends, siblings, or the media (Centers for Disease Control and Prevention 2019). Furthermore, "studies have shown that teens who report talking with their parents about sex are more likely to delay having sex and to use condoms when they do have sex (Markham et al., 2010)." Parents should be aware that the following aspects of communication can have an impact on teen sexual behavior:

- what is said
- how it is said
- how often it is said
- how much teens feel cared for, and understood by, their parents (Jaccard et al., 2002).

IT IS A MYTH THAT TALKING TO YOUNG PEOPLE ABOUT SEX WILL ENCOURAGE THEM TO BECOME SEXUALLY ACTIVE.[11]

Young and old people alike need others they can trust who can guide them in their questioning and development. (Which by the way, never stops happening!) Throughout our lives, our

---

11   If the research is not enough to convince you, let me add that there is no bigger turn off than your parents or guardians talking to you about sex.

sexual attitudes and behaviors will change and evolve. We cannot honestly expect one class, workshop or conversation from when we were kids to satisfy what is ultimately a lifelong journey of questioning and rediscovering sex.

For those who grow up queer, trans, gender nonconforming, intersex or any other marginalized gender or sexual identity, it is not just a matter of an initial awkwardness of talking about sex or bodies. For many, broaching these conversations, even in their households, could threaten their physical and psychological safety.

Beginning to build a chosen family is the first step to having access to the care, support and mentorship that may not have been present growing up.[12] Because our own families may not share our queer identities and may never be able to relate to those specific experiences, our chosen family are often already mentors in our sexual journeys.

By no coincidence you may have grown up in a culture, environment, or household that did not speak openly about sex. Blaming the household you were raised is really the tip of the iceberg in terms of understanding the entire system put in place to disconnect us from holistic and accurate sex education.

With important topics like sex or race, the more comfortable we are talking about the things that matter, the more prepared and equipped we will be able to handle them. You

---

12 A chosen family is made up of people who have intentionally chosen to embrace, nurture, love, and support each other regardless of blood or marriage.

do not need to be teaching a sex-ed class in schools in order to be a mentor to your communities. We are all sexuality educators in varying degrees, even if it's just for ourselves.

Thank you for reading. In my eyes, you have stepped into your own power and have begun unpacking this world for yourself.

NOISE FROM THOSE
IN POWER

———

Decolonizing sex positivity means cultivating a practice of examining whose voices are the loudest and that we hear the most. It means questioning your sources and looking to see if those you are hearing from occupy other places of privilege and power outside of the sexuality space. Are they typically assumed to be the expert? Does their ease of talking about sex mirror any part of their identity?

Because sex is such a stigmatized topic, it makes sense that speaking more openly about it will combat the stigma. I can understand why some people find talking about sex to be such a "freeing" thing. Some might feel as if, "Finally! I am not being punished or silenced about the things that matter to me!"

Decolonizing sex positivity means re-evaluating norms and practices around de-stigmatizing sex. Especially when we live in a country that blindly defaults to values of white patriarchy, we cannot expect the assumed norms and practices of any space to be radically inclusive. Without that re-evaluation, one might assume that spaces where sex is spoken about openly is automatically inclusive and uplifting. But who is creating this space? What are the norms and expectations? Were those norms and expectations communicated and what values informed them?

While it may be tempting to combat stigma with open conversation and dialogue, without a trauma-informed approach that recognizes power and identity to address those questions, people can feel unsafe and excluded. And these "people" in question tend to be those with the least amount of power in the room.

IT IS A MYTH THAT SHARING YOUR SEX STORIES IS NECESSARY TO BE SEX POSITIVE.

A common pitfall of sex positive advocates is adopting a "full charge ahead" mentality to talking about sex. This is just as harmful as the other extreme of perpetuating silence. Being sex positive does not necessarily translate to being comfortable talking publicly about your sex life. In fact, expecting people to share their sex stories and connection to sex openly can be intrusive.

Brené Brown talks about connecting to people through acts of vulnerability. In her book, *Daring Greatly*, she warns against "floodlighting" or when people share stories in a grand gesture without consent or thought of how the massive unloading will impact the other party.

Instead, Brown encourages viewing moments of vulnerability as twinkling lights. Small, vulnerable instances that collectively light up a space.

The same thing can show up when we share our stories about sex.

When we safely share stories of ourselves that relate to sex, sexuality, and relationships with the consent of those around us, real magic can happen. No one knows that better than Brianna Booth. The work she does is all about exploring how people's stories of sex are tied to shame.

MEET BRIANNA BOOTH, FOUNDER AND DIRECTOR OF POSITIVE SEXUALITY AT STANFORD

Brianna Booth is the Director of Positive Sexuality at Stanford University. She earned her PhD in Human Sexuality Studies and a Masters in Applied Positive Psychology at Widener University, focusing her research on the lived experience of sexuality and the skills of navigating it well. Her role as Director of Positive Sexuality is one that she created herself. The position was born out of a need to develop campus-wide programming and resources to start conversations about sexuality.

In our interview, she explained her theory of change and how she got to where she was. Booth says, "I got here because I wanted to make a more thoughtful and compassionate culture around sexuality and the parts that are so easily and quickly judged." Brianna has always thought that sexuality has the potential to trigger shame in the most intense and quickest way possible. Her work welcomes people and their stories exactly as they are: the proud moments and the parts that we are ashamed of.

At Stanford, Brianna leads the program, "Beyond Sex-Ed: Consent & Sexuality at Stanford." Beyond Sex-Ed starts as a storytelling class where students write about their experiences around topics like family, romance, friendship, love, and sex. In the seminar, Booth invites students to talk to one another, share secrets and ultimately get a glimpse into their sexuality journey via storytelling. The class culminates in a beautiful showcase where students share their stories with friends and peers.

At the end of every academic year, a handful of former students from Beyond Sex-Ed are asked to retell their stories for the entire incoming first year and transfer class. Can you imagine that kind of vulnerability? Performing in front of upwards of sixteen hundred people is no easy feat—especially when you're sharing one of the most intimate parts of your life. I would not know. I declined the invitation!

See, I had attended Beyond Sex-Ed as a freshman in 2016 and absolutely hated it! I was so shocked and bewildered to hear people openly share their most personal stories of sex and intimacy. It sparked a deep shame of my own that I did not know existed. I was catapulted into years of grappling with what it meant to be a sexual being. Four years later in the spring of 2020, I enrolled in that same Beyond Sex-Ed course purely for the two units I needed to complete my Theatre and Performing Arts degree. I had no clue of the journey I would find myself on.

Week by week, my classmates and I were asked to dive into questions like, "What was our relationship to hookup culture, and how does it affect us? What did we want out of love, relationship, intimacy? What did sex mean to us?" I had never been asked these questions, let alone asked myself! And thus began a slow and gradual practice of picking up stories of my own, turning them over, and examining them more closely.

I was asked to share my story at the Beyond Sex-Ed showcase, but it was during a time in my life that my world was turning upside down due to the pandemic. Though I did not perform, I went on to write this book, and I recognize the role Beyond Sex-Ed played in that decision.

Brianna's philosophy is mirrored in the objective of the program, which is to humanize sexuality through real people's stories. Brianna says the best way to learn and connect to ourselves and better understand other people is through storytelling.

Brianna laughed mid-conversation in our interview together. "Being a human is hard!"

I laughed with her. She is right. Being a human is not easy. It is not easy to find the middle ground of removing stigma by talking about taboo subjects while also being mindful of the different relationships people have to sex. And it is definitely not easy when we are left to learn this on our own.

I think it is less about finding a "middle ground" or "balance" and more of a dance that we must do—a dance or series of fluid movements in which we navigate the emotional safety of ourselves and others while being aware of the identities we hold and the intention behind our story sharing.

This "dance" should be done to a soundtrack of the voices we hear the least in sexuality spaces. And if we listen closely, over the noise from those in power, this soundtrack will provide the rhythm and beat for us to dance the next steps.

COMPROMISE IS COLONIAL

———

Decolonizing sex positivity means acknowledging the ways colonialism has conditioned us to work toward compromise. Without learning how to create and respect boundaries, we inadvertently compromise our needs and desires.

We speak of consent in a vacuum to college-aged kids who are often learning the word for the first time and understanding it as a binary of "yes" versus "no." For example, "yes" does not mean "always" nor is it unconditional.[13] Little is done to connect topics of consent to day-to-day instances of respecting boundaries or recognizing "micro-violations." An example of a *micro-violation* is a nonconsensual hug or behavior done with any intention that assumes another's consent without asking.[14] When we don't seek consent, we assume another person's feelings, wants and needs. We send

---

13 As Mary Kate Olson says, "No is a complete sentence."
14 Michaela Coel's hit TV show, *I May Destroy You* explicitly shows the ways that micro-violations can show up, even in situations of good intention between friends.

the message that our will and desire is more important than theirs (Sex Positive Families 2020).

Our lessons about consent date back to how you were raised and what you learned about boundaries as a child. From a young age, many of us are encouraged and rewarded for not having physical boundaries with adults. (I.e., "Awww Fatimah is so sweet for always hugging her uncle.") Consent should extend across a lifespan. In order to decolonize sex positivity, we must cultivate practices of age-informed consent.

As we age and our bodies change, so must our understanding and practices of consent. Without the understanding of consent as a lifelong process, we ignore the systemic ways in which violations of consent become embedded in how we work, parent, teach, and love.

Furthermore, the way we teach consent now does not accurately capture the full spectrum of people's experiences. The ages when people are the most sexually active (however they define that for themselves) also varies across their lifespan. For some, the most sexually active part of their life may be well into their seventies. Young kids may enter adulthood without ever learning about consent, leaving them vulnerable to harmful violations. When we have conversations of consent at specific ages, we indirectly signal that consent is only relevant for certain times of our life.

In recent years, I have seen discourse around boundaries as primary ways of navigating and practicing consent. Decolonizing sex positivity means creating cultures of consent that do not solely rely on the individual to uphold. Failures to set proper boundaries are also reflective of societal norms. Boundaries should not be restricted to the expectation that individuals should communicate what they need and want at all times, it should also include larger collective care that creates a norm of being aware of one another.

IT IS A MYTH THAT CONSENT IS SIMPLY ABOUT AGREEING TO HAVE SEX OR NOT.

I remember the summer before my freshman year at Stanford. All first years and transfer students were required to do an online training about consent and sexual assault. It was my first time ever learning the word "consent."

And I was not alone. Many of my friends and peers were not familiar with the word, especially in nonsexual contexts. Thanks to the #MeToo movement, conversations of consent are more commonplace now. Nevertheless, as a society, we should not wait until college to speak deeply about consent with a "one and done" mentality for what should be a lifelong, evolving practice.

Melissa Carnagey from Sex Positive Families makes it clear to families that conversations about sex and consent should happen in the home. They emphasize in their workshops that sex should feel good and that it happens between consenting adults. They say, "Consent means permission. When there is not consent that is a crime or abuse."

Compromising on our needs and pleasure stems from white colonialism and patriarchy. Control and power start at a young age in a culture that affirms a sense of superiority over kids.[15] While the origins of this relationship of caretaker and child exists for good reason (specifically, safety) as children mature there is no formal renegotiation of that power.[16]

"Instead of training children to meet the expectations of adults, we should be training adults to meet the psychological, emotional, and development needs of children," says teacher, Zoe Tolman. Growing up, there's a real sense you are being controlled, and you must behave in accordance with adults' expectations. An example of such is the expectation of not having physical boundaries. As a result, moments of non-consent are normalized. (i.e., "You're so friendly for letting me pinch your cheeks.")

Melissa Carnagey talks openly about the horrors of seeing a screaming child sit on Santa's lap for pictures. Carnagey says, "It is not cute. It is unsafe." They challenge us even further saying, "What early messages are we sending by forcing a young person onto the lap of a stranger, simply for a photo op? Creating a safer, consent-conscious next generation requires us to re-evaluate norms and traditions such as this."

Ultimately, creating a conscious consent culture begins with communication. At every age, we should all be getting in the habit of asking for permission. And isn't it a beautiful thing

---

15 Superiority over kids is also a colonial belief.

16 Especially in situations when children are in stages of earlier development or living with different abilities that require adults to make decisions on their behalf. One practice of consent could look like walking through intentions with open communication. Then paying attention to non-verbal cues is important, being ready to make adjustments or stop as needed in response.

when people can consent to everyday encounters? Before it has anything to do with sex, families can create a consent-conscious home by how they interact with each other. Here are some examples:

"May I take a picture of/with you?"

"Would you like a hug?"

"Can I have a bite of your snack?"

"Is it okay if I tell what you shared with me?"

"Would you like help with that?"

"They said stop, so that's enough."

"May I post this picture online for others to see?"

"May I borrow your..."

"No? Okay, I respect that."

"Are you comfortable with me being this close?" (Sex Positive Families 2021)

Some may argue, "Why do I have to ask permission from a child?" or "They're MY child, and until they're on their own in this world, they do what I say."

These attitudes condition children to be accustomed to being controlled, operating out of a sense of obligation, and being less able to assertively communicate their needs or boundaries without fear. It can prime them to be victims or oppressors within their future relationships. When kids turn eighteen, there suddenly is an expectation of them being an adult with the consciousness and skills of consent that may have never been explicitly taught. Families can practice power sharing in the household in ways that are sustainable and foster confidence in children's autonomy. This does not mean you do not have limits or guidance for your kids. Kids don't want our power; they want their own power.[17]

When we look at ageism in the United States and the ways that many people's place in society is shunned as they grow older, I see opportunity for growth in cultivating a practice of age-informed consent.

Elderly adults can often have their voices silenced as they require more support from healthcare professionals or family members. Especially in the United States, institutions are built in a way that infantilize the elderly and restrict their agency. In the words of Chloe Kirlew, a Holistic Health and Consent Educator, "Depending on their social privilege, race and mobility, some elderly people have their choices, boundaries and experiences invalidated."

And of course, these harmful experiences of ageism come back to capitalism as capitalism dictates that the worth of human beings is based off their productivity. So, toward the end of people's lives as they age, they are treated as disposable.

---

17 Radicalfamilies and latinxparent are Instagram accounts devoted to the deconstructing power dynamic in families. I would recommend them.

One of the consequences of this is less availability of education and resources around building safe, consensual communities for elderly folks. I want to work toward a future in which boundary setting and consent are recognized as lifelong skills and are taught as such. I want to work toward the truth that your body may change but your worth does not. I want to work toward a future where people at different life stages, existing in different bodies and who have different needs, are supported and respected by all.

PLEASURE IS NOT
A LUXURY

———

Decolonizing sex positivity means cultivating a deep understanding of the fact that pleasure is not and should not be a
luxury. It begins with tracing this idea that pleasure should
be a luxury to a tenet of white supremacy that asserts that
only "those in power have a right to emotional and psychological comfort (Jones & Okun 2001)."[18]

Institutions, media movements, and societal reinforcement
signal that prioritizing sexual pleasure is frivolous and/or
hedonistic. In order to be sex positive, you must reject sex
negativity. Sex negativity implies "human sexuality is inherently dangerous and overindulgent and must be contained in
a majority of circumstances (Johnson 2019)." Sex negativity
"incites fear, restriction, and polarization" and only encourages sex that is expressed in a specific way, within a narrow
range of demographics (Johnson 2019). Much of traditional
sex-education centers white, able-bodied, thin, heterosexual,

———

18   Pleasure is larger than merely experiencing orgasms as will be discussed
     in the next chapter.

cis-gendered people. This is called *pleasure bias*. Pleasure bias dictates who we think deserves pleasure and who we think should be having sex.

For a long time, I thought—why should *I* write this book? Surely many people are more experienced and knowledgeable. I realized that the reason why I know so little was not incidental or through some fault of my own. It is because queer Black and brown communities are often left out of conversations about sex and pleasure.

Sex is a luxury that we are made to believe was not intended for us. Television and media teach us that only certain people have sex and experience pleasure.[19] We do not see poor people, fat people, older people, disabled people, or people with STIs having pleasurable sex. And when it comes to people of color, especially women of color, we are conditioned to see our pleasure as a burden. When we center on those deemed "less worthy" of sex, we are able to work toward a future where pleasure is seen and understood as a right.

---

19 I would be remiss to not mention main stream pornography when I refer to where and how we learn about who we imagine to be having good sex. Marija Kamena, a medical student at Stanford University, says in their workshop titled "Trans Talks: Trans Inclusive Safer Sex" in partnership with San Mateo Pride Center and the Stanford LGBTQ+ Health Program, "Do not compare yourself or your experiences to porn. It is a performance spliced to show the best parts according to some random cis-gender straight guy out there."

IT IS A MYTH THAT PLEASURE SHOULD BE A LUXURY. IT IS A MYTH THAT ONLY SKINNY, STRAIGHT, WHITE, ABLE-BODIED, AND CIS-GENDERED PEOPLE ARE HAVING SEX AND EXPERIENCING PLEASURE. Capitalism reinforces things like rest, safety, and pleasure as conditional luxuries. Because our bodies are treated as tools for production, we learn we should be compensated for what we produce, when in reality we all deserve and are entitled to such comforts. Adrienne Maree Brown states the following about pleasure, "Part of the reason so few of us have a healthy relationship with pleasure is because a small minority of our species hoards the excess of resources, creating a false scarcity and then trying to sell us joy, sell us back to ourselves (Brown 2019)." Brown continues by pointing out that white people and men especially feel entitled to pleasure. When Brown speaks of pleasure, it is a vision of pleasure separate from the "spoils of capitalism (Brown, 2019)." The kind of pleasure Adrienne and I are talking about is the nourishing, joyful pleasure that awakens our bodies and hearts to living. This pleasure is rooted in abundance—a far cry from the feel-good thrills that temporarily appease us whenever we come up for air in this scarcity driven, capitalistic hamster wheel society we live in.

Because the status we have in our society is one of sub-version (resulting in misogynoir), many Black women are conditioned to view themselves as undeserving of pleasure. This originates from the regulation of Black women's bodies through slavery in a postcolonial country—"stolen people on stolen land," as contributing editor of Consciously Decolonizing, Adele Thomas says.

This is why Black feminism is a tool for unpacking pleasure as a luxury and understanding sexual liberation as a pathway to Black liberation. The theory is grounded on the unique experience of Black women and puts forward a way of thinking that acknowledges the ways privilege and power can manifest for different identities. The digital platform, Afrosexology, creates spaces online and in real life for Black people to discuss sexual exploration and liberation. Throughout my research, Afrosexology was a resource that continually affirmed my work and charged my writing. One of the cofounders, Dalychia Saah shares openly about her reasons for entering the sex-ed space. In the following excerpt, she questions the messages she received as a Black woman growing up and living in the United States.

> How is it that white men systematically raped black women and faced no penalty but then lynched so many black boys and men under the accusation of raping white women? Why did I grow up not seeing any public displays of affection in my African household? Why was I acting fast and he just being a boy? Why was I told Black people have rhythm and then chastised for dancing in a way that felt natural to my spirit? Why was I responsible for our chastity? Why was the horniness that came with my puberty not seen as lady like? Why is it that we're seen as hypersexual? That our men are reduced to a big penis, our women to big butts? Why do I feel shame when I orgasm? Are we being impacted from past trauma? How do we heal from this trauma? Do we love ourselves? Do we feel like there's something to love? Do we love one another? What is love (Saah 2015)?

These questions weighed heavily on Dalychia's heart and led her to shy away from talking about sex. She says, "I felt like discussing sexuality was a luxury granted only to white and privileged people. Because when Blacks as a global community are struggling with hunger, financial stability, constant violence, just trying to survive; who has the time or energy to sit around and talk about sex (Saah 2015)?"

Reading Dalychia's words for the first time sent shivers down my back. She had managed to capture the same pondering I had carried for years. When we understand capitalism's hold on our ideas of pleasure, we can deeply appreciate that sexual liberation is an integral piece of Black liberation and thus, our collective liberation. Systems that dehumanize people leverage the stripping of their sexual identity to do so.[20] When we treat pleasure as a right, we can appropriately acknowledge and address when human rights violations have been made.

Equitable societies are built on honoring individuals rights so that everyone (in theory) has equal access to a higher quality of life. In October of 2019, participants of the 24th World Congress of the World Association for Sexual Health (WAS) convened in Mexico City to rally around pleasure being seen as a right. They agreed to the following six declarations:

---

20 What better case study than the legacy of American slavery and mass incarceration in the United States.

DECLARATION ON SEXUAL PLEASURE

Mexico City, October 15, 2019

The participants of the 24th World Congress of the World Association for Sexual Health

RECOGNIZE that:

1. The possibility of having pleasurable and safe sexual experiences free of discrimination, coercion, and violence is a fundamental part of sexual health and well-being for all.
2. Access to sources of sexual pleasure is part of human experience and subjective well-being.
3. Sexual pleasure is a fundamental part of sexual rights as a matter of human rights.
4. Sexual pleasure includes the possibility of diverse sexual experiences.
5. Sexual pleasure shall be integrated into education, health promotion, and service delivery, research, and advocacy in all parts of the world.
6. The programmatic inclusion of sexual pleasure to meet individuals' needs, aspirations, and realities ultimately contributes to global health and sustainable development and it should require comprehensive, immediate, and sustainable action.

In my eyes, the following stipulations are the bread and butter of explaining what it means to live in a society that values sexual pleasure as a right. The definition of "sexual pleasure" as stated in this declaration links pleasure to sexual rights and sexual health based in "self-determination, consent, safety, privacy, confidence, communication, and the ability to negotiate with partners." A society that values pleasure as a human right reflects that in law and policy, comprehensive sexuality education and public health. Public consciousness can only shift when these types of measures are taken.

The next chapter, *Pleasure as a measure of freedom,* is the closest I have gotten to mapping out what it means to support and live out pleasure as our birthright.

OUR BODIES TEACH US WHAT FREEDOM FEELS LIKE

Our bodies teach us what freedom feels like.

—ADRIENNE MAREE BROWN, PLEASURE ACTIVISM

How does white supremacy feel in your body?

I was asked this in a workshop in September 2020. To answer, I thought of the feeling of walking through mud. Or breathing through a straw. White supremacy makes me feel ten times smaller than my actual size. You may be wondering, "Wait Mo—what are you talking about? White supremacy is about social oppression. What does it have to do with a 'feeling in the body?'"

Decolonizing sex positivity means recognizing the body as the main site of oppression in Western society. There is a real consequence to your mental and physical health in being born on stolen land in a country with a history and current reality of white supremacy.

Because grind culture dictates that we push ourselves further, work harder, and ignore the needs of our body for the sake of productivity, messages around sex and sexuality have the potential to mirror a similar sentiment. It shows up in our instinct to accept pain, discomfort, and micro-violations in and out of the bedroom. It shows up for those who convince themselves they do not deserve to feel good during sex. It shows up in the orgasm gap when women, femmes, and non-men prioritize the pleasure of their partners over their own. It shows up in the resulting sexual trauma that is compounded when these forces collide, and our bodies absorb the impact.

But decolonizing sex positivity also means accepting that the body can simultaneously be a site of liberation. Hence, this chapter is named after a quote by Adrienne Maree Brown from her book *Pleasure Activism*. Our bodies *can* teach us what freedom feels like. If the body does indeed "keep score" and can be the place where trauma resides, it can also be our map to find our way toward healing. In the words of Jezz Chung, "Decolonizing the mind and reprogramming over the imprints of white supremacist ideology isn't a single action. It's a complete shift in the way we think. It's also a life-long practice. And while the mind is a starting point, Indigenous and ancestral wisdom always lead back to the body."

Many Black and brown radicals and thought leaders of the twenty-first century have been openly addressing the ways that social oppression impacts the physical body and mind. This chapter is a drop in the ocean compared to the literature that exists in this realm. I recommend Adrienne Maree Brown's book, *Pleasure Activism* and Sonya Renee Taylor's, *The Body is Not an Apology* among others to continue your learning.

I refer to different situations and circumstances that ultimately inform the experience I describe as the "feeling of white supremacy in my body." Whether it's decades of working in white dominated workspaces and academic settings or being held to the standard of whiteness as a marker of success, the years' worth of trauma impacts my body in the way I breathe, show up and navigate the world.

The rest of the chapter continues to direct our attention to the body—our bodies. While we gain an incredible amount of information from the ways people interact with our bodies (sexual and nonsexual), it is not compulsory that pleasure be tied to other people.

THAT IS WHY IT IS A MYTH THAT WE CANNOT EXPERIENCE PLEASURE IF WE ARE NOT HAVING SEXUAL EXPERIENCES WITH OTHER PEOPLE.

Because I write about "honoring your body" in this chapter, I want to be mindful of the different relationships people have with their bodies. I often see social media accounts that center body positivity exclusively around masturbation and a directionless idea of simply "loving yourself."

As I mention at the start of the book, this type of messaging risks doing more harm. It often disregards the complex histories of shame that continue to be reinforced by culture and society. Irrespective of shame, these messages may simply not resonate with everyone.

Many of us, especially communities of color, have been conditioned to be disconnected from our bodies. It is by no fault of our own, especially where there is no education around an understanding of inherent worth.[21] Many of our first relationships with our bodies was corrective. We are always trying to fix things: "Something's wrong. It must be corrected," or "I must deny things that give me pleasure."

We are thrust into a society sending us messages that we're not good enough, we are not wanted, we are not desired, and that in turn, leads to a constant policing of our bodies, thoughts, opportunities, and our trajectory.

Self-policing means we begin to restrict our own bodies based on what we learn is socially acceptable. As Steve Biko, Black liberation fighter, memorably wrote in 1971, "The most potent weapon in the hands of the oppressor is the mind of the oppressed (Biko 1971).

Self-policing, unfortunately, is a perfect example of that "potent weapon." In the words of Dr. Tracie Gilbert,

> *When you look at racialization and what that has meant, it started with the bodies we had. When colonizers came, they needed to regulate [Black people's] bodies and so by extension that included regulating our*

---

21   "Inherent worth" does not exist under capitalism as it contradicts worth being tied to production.

[sexual identities]. They didn't want you dancing on the boat. They didn't want you having sex with nobody, at least not in the ways you were doing. They didn't want you dressing [. . .] or doing your hair in a certain way. It was all about body regulation until it became a matter of self-policing.

In my interview with Dr. Gilbert, she described how that history of self-policing shows up today in commands we were indoctrinated with at a young age. "Keep your legs closed. Don't be chewing your gum like that. Learn to close your mouth. You're talking too much."

Dr. Gilbert continues: "And so when you become a good girl like I did, you master that. That's how you succeed. You master keeping yourself composed [...] and restricted. I've been doing this work for ten years, and a lot of that work is unlearning. Unlearning all of it."

Self-policing demonstrates one way that hating your body becomes a learned behavior. It can feel like you are not your own. Dalychia Saah of Afrosexology reminds us that this is why immersing our bodies in feelings of pleasure and love is an act of rebellion, "especially in a system that would have us internalize and externalize self-hate (Saah 2015)." Because if this constructed White supremacist system was built and continues to operate on the denial of our humanity and exploitation of our Black bodies, reclaiming our bodies is pivotal in the destruction of it all (Saah 2015).

BODY POSITIVITY & FATPHOBIA

Our relationship to bodies, not just our own, are laced with fatphobia and able-ist beliefs.

Since being "inclusive" and "intersectional" is trendy right now, I've noticed how vague philosophies on body positivity have also risen to popularity. Fatphobia is rampant in these portrayals of body positivity. I sat down to interview Jordan Simone (@jordxnsimone), a Black queer influencer on Tiktok who makes videos about race, sexuality and identity. One of her most viral videos garnered a response from Lizzo. At the time, a popular trend on Tiktok (a social app that allows users to make short videos) involved users videotaping their body at different angles and hash tagging "body positivity." Simone points out that much of the messaging in those videos still ascribes to the idea that there is such a thing as a perfect or an imperfect body.

In an interview with *Vogue* magazine, Lizzo says:

> *Now, you look at the hashtag "body positive," and you see smaller-framed girls, curvier girls. Lotta white girls. And I feel no ways about that because inclusivity is what my message is always about. I'm glad that this conversation is being included in the mainstream narrative. What I don't like is how the people that this term was created for are not benefiting from it. Girls with back fat, girls with bellies that hang, girls with thighs that aren't separated, that overlap. Girls with stretch marks. You know, girls who are in the eighteen-plus club (Paris 2020).*

Not only has Lizzo brought attention to the effects of body positivity becoming mainstream, but according to Simone, Lizzo also challenges the idea that there's an imperfect body at all. Simone says, "Because many people can more or less fluctuate between the imperfect and perfect additions of beauty, we have a harder time accepting our body in its "imperfect way." Because fat people are deemed imperfect [by societal norms] all the time, they're having a conversation about dismantling the idea of a perfect body all together." Simone continues by saying, "Skinny people are talking about acceptance. Fat people are talking about liberation."

Sonya Renee Taylor, author of *The Body Is Not an Apology*, writes that the blossoming movement treats body positivity as a trophy we can only receive once we've reached some state of self-love enlightenment (Taylor 2018). "Our presumed failures at attaining some body-love nirvana becomes just another source of shame," concludes Taylor.

After the emergence of the body positivity movement, body neutrality was offered as an alternative approach. Instead of focusing on loving your body no matter what, body neutrality takes a neutral perspective toward your body, "meaning that you do not have to cultivate a love for your body or feel that you have to love your body every day. You may not always love your body, but you may still live happily and appreciate everything your body can do (Fuller 2021)." Though body neutrality is offered as an alternative to body positivity, both mindsets can be practiced together.

Perhaps we would understand our bodies better as parts of the universe with the answer not being to always try to vaguely love them. There are other verbs I can conjure. We can appreciate our bodies. Take care of them. Normalize them. Feed them. Nurture them. Adore them. We can feel neutral about them. We can change our bodies. We can learn more about them.

It is no surprise that these expansive and affirming messages that are just now arriving to mainstream audiences have been the lifework and practice of queer and disabled people for centuries.

DISABILITY JUSTICE AS A TOOL OF LIBERATION

I met Mari Wrobi, a queer, nonbinary intersex Latinx advocate who works with queer youth, at the 2020 Global Sexual Health World Day Conference where they spoke on a panel about barriers to pleasure, specifically for the intersex community.

When I interviewed them, they spoke about the necessity of listening to their body. "As somebody who is intersex, who is trans, who is queer, who exists at the various intersections of all these identities, I think just plainly listening to my body is a lesson that I've had to learn. It can be a hard lesson because you so want to be what you might see in other people."

When I asked Mari what they would tell their younger self, they answered smiling:

"I would have told my younger self, just be okay in your body and listen to yourself. Follow your own intuition—your own feelings. You don't have to try so hard to be something else.

As an intersex person so much of the barriers to sex and pleasure [come from] the traumatic nature that we have with our bodies. Things like medical procedures, surgeries and doctors are tied to many intersex experiences. It's a lot of learning the economy of my body after it was taken away in other ways."

I loved what they said about learning the economy of the body, especially after it has been taken away. It reminds me of Adrienne Maree Brown's words, "No matter how much has been taken from you, reclamation is possible. There are many paths back to yourself."

Another panelist on "Barriers to Pleasure," Dr. Sabitha Pillai-Friedman spoke about barriers to pleasure for cancer survivors.[22] According to Dr. Pillai-Friedman, doctors and healthcare professionals' feelings of embarrassment sometimes stop them from discussing sexual side effects of medical treatment with their patients. Can you imagine? The very person who is hugely implicated in your health being too embarrassed or confused to bring up pertinent information about your body as it relates to sex. Dr. Pillai-Friedman adds that especially in the medical field, sexual function is prioritized over sexual pleasure. An agreement amongst the panelists was that too often, people's assumptions about pleasure cause pain.

---

22 Dr. Pillai-Friedman has over twenty-five years of experience in providing psychotherapy and teaching, as well as in training psychotherapists and sex therapists. She operates under her own practice, Rittenhouse Relationship and Sexual Health Center.

People like Mari and others who have spent their lives in and proximal to the healthcare system know very well about the insidious ways that white supremacy and ableism emerge and manifest. For many disabled queer, trans and intersex people, their bodies are inherently political by virtue of existing. In the words of Patty Berne, Sins Invalid cofounder and director:

> *The histories of white supremacy and ableism are inextricably intertwined, both forged in the crucible of colonial conquest and capitalist domination. One cannot look at the history of US slavery, the stealing of Indigenous land, and US imperialism without seeing the way that white supremacy leverages ableism to create a subjugated "other" that is deemed lest worthy/ abled/smart/capable.*
>
> *We cannot comprehend ableism without grasping its interrelation with heteropatriarchy, white supremacy, colonialism and capitalism. Each system benefits from extracting profits and status from the subjugated "other." Five hundred plus years of violence against Black and brown communities includes five hundred plus years of bodies and minds deemed "dangerous" by being nonnormative.*
>
> *Disabled people of the global majority—Black and brown people—share common ground confronting and subverting colonial powers in our struggle for life and justice (Piepzna-Samarasinha, 2018).*

Leah Lakshmi's book, *Care Work: Dreaming Disability Justice* delves into Disability Justice, a movement that centers the lives and leadership of sick and disabled queer, trans, Black and brown people, to develop a toolkit for creating sustainable communities of liberation where no one is left behind (Piepzna-Samarasinha, 2018). Disability Justice is a critical framework for us to learn how to teach our bodies what freedom feels like. I believe the tenets of Disability Justice can be a compass for us to find and follow those paths back to ourselves.

I especially love Alison Kafer's book, *Feminist, Queer, Crip* as it comes from a Disability Justice perspective and defies the white supremacist norm of always moving and working in a state of urgency (Jones & Okun, 2001). In the first chapter of her book, Kafer writes about "crip time" as a reorientation to time. "Crip time" is an examination of how expectations of "how long things take" are based on very particular minds and bodies (Kaker, 2013). In other words, our society defaults to time as experienced by a "productive" neurotypical, able-bodied people. Kafer continues, "We can understand the flexibility of crip time as being not only an accommodation to those who need 'more' time but also, and perhaps especially, a challenge to normative and normalizing expectations of pace and scheduling. Rather than bend disabled bodies and minds to meet the clock, crip time bends the clock to meet disabled bodies and minds" (Kafer, 2013). In this way, moving at our own pace and understanding "crip time" is in of itself, is a decolonial practice we can use to honor our bodies.

HONORING YOUR BODY

Recognizing and honoring your body's needs is a practice and skill that gets better with time and has to start small. Not even with anything sexual. Consider, what is your body telling you at this very moment? Do you want to keep reading? Go to the bathroom? Take a nap? Stretch?

When we can get in the practice of claiming our needs, it is far less intimidating and daunting to tune in to our body's response to pleasure. Starting off small is important because there is that possibility of triggering our bodies to feel unsafe. One of Afrosexology's webinars, *How to Put on a Masturbation Show*, is designed to help you learn about anatomy, tips, and tricks for self-pleasuring while exploring the stages of arousing your erotic self. In the workshop, Dalychia says, "We often expect other people to meet our needs, and we're not even meeting our own needs. [...] Learning to be more in tune with our body helps us to trust it. We're listening to it, so when our other needs come up, our sexual and erotic needs, there is less judgment. [...] Our body is learning that we are in relationship with it."

In the words of Dr. Nikki Coleman, "It's one thing to say, 'I want soup and salad for lunch.' It's another thing to order specific items off the menu, like the tomato bisque and kale avocado salad." With practice, we will have the language and confidence for expressing what feels good to us. And those things will change as we change, and our bodies change. With those changes, we have the opportunity to continue learning. Get to know how your body says "yes" and how it says "no." Getting really good at it now can help on that journey throughout your lifetime.

Decolonizing practices are rooted in noticing the somatic and using it as a source of knowledge rather than what is solely considered "rational." This can be transformative as we live in a society that uplifts grind culture and tells us to push through and produce. Our bodies can act as evidence in our journey to healing and explorations of pleasure.

QUEERING SEX
POSITIVITY

———

It is tempting to believe that sex positivity is a sign of the times and a reflection of modernity. The literature shows the opposite. Communities of color around the globe have had praxis in healthy models of sexuality that acknowledge spectrums and fluidity around aspects of sex.

Decolonizing sex positivity means understanding sex and sexuality within the tenets of queer theory. This means that we acknowledge that colonization enforced the gender binary and disconnected Indigenous knowledge and ways of being that were inherently gender affirming and sex positive.

I think about the erasure of prevailing examples and demonstrations of healthy sexuality that were not documented on account of oral traditions being the principal vehicle of culture sharing.

What has shifted in recent decades after the internet was "invented" has been the reclaiming of information pertinent to progressive views on sex. Whether through social media accounts, community-based research reports or books, we (those of us who recognize the systems we are under) have become a generation of Sankofa's—a flock of mythical birds flying forward with our heads turned backwards.

Being sex positive means you accept others' sexual practices, as long as the participants consent and feel safe, without moral judgment. This means accepting sexual behaviors that might be different from your own as well as accepting others' sexual orientations and lifestyles without judgment. A decolonial framework works in tandem with queer theory by honoring the expansiveness of our lives. We question and challenge not only the gender binary but all binaries.

Compulsory heterosexuality is having straightness (or heteronormativity) be the set norm that everyone is forced to abide by. It is harmful to queer, trans, and/or non-cisgender folk as it erases and demonizes these identities while simultaneously trying to force a system where they must perform straightness and cisness (Wynne 2021).

"The control over bodies and sexualities is inherent to the process of capital accumulation and 'love' turns into an institution that makes care work seem like a natural responsibility that women should bear," says Tica Moreno in their writing, *Women and Gender Nonconforming bodies in Resistance* (Moreno 2021). Heteronormativity is used as "political regime" because 1) it imposes sexualities that are orientated toward the social reproduction of capital (in other words, cis heterosexuality is in service of reproduction) and 2) creates a "manipulation of desires" that essentially streamlines people into opting into heterosexual relationships regardless of whether or not they truly desire to do so (Moreno 2021).

The terms of compulsory heterosexuality are congruent with the aims of white supremacy because it enforces a specific way of being that removes choice and autonomy. In their beautifully poignant and colorful book, *Beyond the Gender Binary,* Alok Vaid Menon declares, "Power can be defined as the ability to make a particular perspective seem universal. Control is how power maintains itself; anyone who expresses another perspective is punished."

Queerness is all about expressing different perspectives. In a heteronormative culture, queerness is positioned as opposite of straightness, *but* queerness is also characterized by deviance—a deviance from the norm. When we "queer" sex positivity, we open up the possibilities for people to consider who they are and who they want to be outside of the compulsory gender and sexuality norms of our society. An unknown author says, "Queerness itself isn't just about who we are attracted to or how we identify our gender. It is about choosing our internal truths over the definitions the external world places on us, again and again throughout the course of our lives."

I wonder then, for you reader, what are your internal truths?

IT IS A MYTH THAT PEOPLE WHO DO NOT IDENTIFY AS QUEER CANNOT EXPLORE THEIR SEXUALITY.

Exploring one's sexuality can be understood as exploring what sex and our identity mean to us outside of the script we've been taught. Because of that deviance, exploring and understanding our sexuality in a radical way challenges binary norms set by colonialism.

IT IS A MYTH THAT "TRUE SEX" ONLY INVOLVES PENIS AND VAGINA INTERCOURSE.

Queering sex positivity means expanding our definitions of what sex is. When I write from a place of freedom, I define sex to be any meaningful experience of pleasure. When we get rid of the "constructs" of our definition of sex, how can it offer permission to explore outside those bounds as well?

Sexuality is more than just having different kinds of sex. Lotus Laine, an activist, adult film producer and porn star says, "The lack of comprehensive sex-ed that includes all aspects of queer sexuality and gender expression, coupled with a lack of media displaying sex and sensuality between same sex partners contributes to cis-gender heterosexual people's extreme, circus-like intrigue into the way queer folks have sex."

George Johnson echoes this when they recount how funny it is that in grade school when schools start doing sex education, not only do they not teach about same sex, they also don't teach about things like anal sex. Johnson exclaims, "And heterosexual couples also have anal sex! So, it's just ignored. The full spectrum of how we have sex is simply ignored and not taught in a way that is actually conducive or healthy for any young adult who's actually going to engage in sex. And if we're not going to teach it to them, how do you think they're going to find out? And I think the primary source is porn. A lot of kids find out about sex and unfortunately romanticize sex through what they see in porn and then try to enact it and perform in that way. And porn is not a real portrayal of what actual sex looks like and feels like."

Queering sex positivity also means acknowledging mindsets and intentions that we unconsciously bring into the bedroom. I wonder: In what ways do capitalist ideologies and tendencies rear their heads in how we as a society conceptualize "good sex" or being sex positive? How we define "success" and "successful" people absolutely comes into play with sex.

In their book, Laziness Does Not Exist, Devon Price, PhD writes about the "laziness lie" (which tells us we are not working or learning hard enough) and how it can infiltrate our sex lives. Price says, "The laziness lie says that if you're not working toward a goal during sex (giving someone what they want or having an orgasm) and if you're not achieving those goals (orgasms, erections, wetness) then sexual encounters are unsuccessful" (Price 2021). When sex becomes another task to complete or skill to excel at, sexual pleasure satisfaction drops exponentially (Price 2021). What could sex look like without the end goal being climax or orgasm? How could that expand our imaginations and invite playfulness?

Mari Wrobi offers insight when they say, "It's so important for people who are queer, trans, and intersex to be able to explore pleasure that exists in other ways." Pleasure mapping is one way to deconstruct what we think pleasure should look and feel like. Pleasure mapping emphasizes exploring outside the genitals to see how other body parts react or feel when stimulated—from the back of your knee to the curve of your ear to the side of your cheek. Pleasure mapping is a practice of queering sex in a practical way. The following is meant to be an offering to get you thinking of other ways you can map pleasure onto your experiences in ways you may have not considered:

- Revisit sex education resources as an adult, check out my resources and appendix for suggestions.
- Learn about how different cultures geographically and throughout different time periods engaged in sex and romance.
- Consider what brings you pleasure in your everyday life and if those things could map onto sex (i.e., aftercare, pleasure products, aromatherapy, etc.)
- Have conversations about sex which can be anonymized online or in-person with friends and peers[23]
- Consume media that talks about sex and romance, including those in nonsexual contexts (e.g., Netflix shows, sex-ed books, YouTube tutorials, etc.).
- Engage in movement and mediation that centers pleasure in sexual and nonsexual contexts (e.g., sensual art, mindful movement, dancing, laughter, etc.).
- Journal and workshop about things that make you feel good and things that do not.[24]

---

23 For example, Dr. Nikki Coleman offers "girlfriend gatherings" where she coaches and facilitates groups of friends talking about sex.

24 Afrosexology and other digital resources offer specific workbooks if you'd like more guidance.

LIBERATION:
A CUSTOM FIT

———

Even after completing this book, I hesitate to call myself sexually liberated. I know I am sex positive, but to go a step further and claim being sexually liberated sounds incredibly intimidating and a bit raunchy. *Sexually liberated.* For some, those words immediately bring up thoughts of hook up culture, "wild women," and casual sex. For this reason, being sexually liberated can carry negative connotations that not everyone wants to be associated with. To claim to be sexually liberated is no easy feat.

IT IS A MYTH THAT SEXUAL LIBERATION IS ENGAGING IN CASUAL SEX AND/OR HAVING MULTIPLE SEXUAL PARTNERS. IT IS ALSO A MYTH THAT SEXUAL LIBERATION IS JUST FOR WOMEN.
Sexual liberation can start with an acknowledgment and understanding of the way that the types of social oppression we defined in the first chapter of this book all inform our connection to sex. Both sex positivity and sexual liberation are often confused to mean being pro-sex or not. While

having multiple partners or engaging in casual sex *can* be one person's approach to sexual liberation, it is not the only approach. In fact, there is no one right answer. Decolonizing sex positivity means recognizing we all have our different definitions of sexual liberation because it is informed by the intersectional identities we hold and the experiences we have.

From survivors to women from culturally conservative backgrounds to religious believers to trans women, the choice to say you're sexually liberated may not be enough or what you even want. That is why I say that liberation must be a "custom fit." A custom fit means acknowledging that what empowers one person may not empower another. We should continue to question how the sex positive movement can become more inclusive and fluid amongst different groups—especially non-men. But, if at the end of that interrogation, there is not a united collective unanimously embracing "sexual liberation," perhaps then it can be an opportunity to examine if we are genuinely doing anything beyond inclusion for the sake of inclusion.

I think back to Jezz Chung's words that I included in the beginning of the book and how they urge us to not be intimidated out of using words like "liberation" and "decolonizing." They remind us that it is okay if these concepts feel overwhelming. It does not mean we should let it stop us from putting those concepts into practice. I also don't want us to be caught in semantics. It is less about the words and phrasing we use and all about the ideas and messages we convey.

You may have another word or feeling for what I call liberation. You can try on this word (or other words!) until it fits well and brings you joy. From there, you can consider sharing it in your spaces and networks if you feel safe doing so. And remember, if you have yet to encounter the right language, know that creating new language is pivotal as you imagine new worlds and ways of being.

Decolonizing sex positivity also means recognizing how deeply sex negativity penetrates into our daily lives affecting everyone, with some being disproportionately affected. This means you can read every book, listen to every podcast and cultivate all your relationships so you are surrounded by healthy models of sexuality and sex positivity and STILL struggle with feelings of disempowerment and shame. Asking women and gender nonconforming people to simply work to "be empowered" places centuries of patriarchal oppression on their own behaviors and can inadvertently place the blame on the individual. While we are ultimately responsible for our own actions, much of our experiences of shame and disempowerment regarding sex can be traced back to cultures of control and supremacy.

In the words of sex educator, Ev'Yan Whitney, "It [sexual liberation] is about getting to the root of how white supremacist patriarchal capitalism dislocates us from our power, our pleasure, our bodily autonomy. And it's only in working to excavate that root and tending to our personal healing that lasting sexual liberation can happen. We need sex education because those systems of oppression exist. So, the work must always have a foundation in the commitment of uprooting those systems. Otherwise, what is it for?"

I appreciate how Whitney makes the distinction between personal healing and the work of uprooting the systems in place that disconnect us from ourselves. These processes are not the same thing, yet they are interwoven in complex and nuanced ways. It can be likened to the work of healthcare professionals seeing individual patients and the public health domain that has a big picture focus on general health determinants.

Ev'Yan Whitney is a sexuality doula who helps women and femme-identifying folks step out of shame, fear, and trauma and into sexual liberation. They are also the founder of *The Sensual Self,* a podcast series about the journey of their clients to becoming sexually liberated women.[25] Whitney knows better than anyone that liberation and empowerment are not a one size fits all. In fact, everyone is entitled to complete freedom when it comes to defining who they are as a sexual being. Sex, connection, love, and intimacy can be practiced differently. The pressure of conformity is a nefarious attribute of white supremacy, which aligns with binary thinking or the pressure of having to fit into a specific narrative.

We know that decolonizing sex positivity means you are able to challenge antiquated and oppressive notions that lead people to being shamed for desiring and/or having pleasurable sex. Instead, you encourage those of all genders to seek to understand their own sexuality and engage in relationships that honor and affirm their desires.

---

25 formerly known as *The Sexually Liberated Woman Podcast*

For some, being sexually liberated has more to do with understanding your identity in relation to those who came before you. Marissa Floro, a sexuality educator at Stanford University, says that sexual liberation comes down to connecting to ancestry.

"I think that liberation, at least in my personal life, has come from this idea of connecting to ancestry [and] connecting to a cultural tradition that is beyond this current white supremacist colonized version of it. [...] Thinking of how much of our own sexual ancestry has been taken from us, in my mind, is pretty liberating (Floro 2020)."

Dr. Inge Hansen, the standing director of the Weiland Initiative as well as the director of Well Being at Stanford University, chimes in on the vastness of what sexual liberation can mean and how it can be harmful to compare our experiences of liberation.

In our interview, she emphasizes the difference between sex positivity and sexual liberation. She describes liberation as an act of being freed or creating freedom after some experience of confinement or bondage.

She says truthfully, "I like the phrase [sexually liberated]. I love the word 'liberation' because it speaks beyond a term like positivity, which I think doesn't always address the struggle. [Sex positivity] can sound more like something you can decide to be whereas sexual liberation acknowledges that we're coming from white supremacy and colonialism and a history of customs, cultures, and restraints that are like shackles that we're trying to break down."

When it comes to comparison, however, we have seen the term "sexually liberated" be weaponized. Dr. Hansen expresses this worry. "I want to make sure that because of that struggle, we're not getting into that place of judgment of like, oh this person's more liberated than this person. I get worried about the culture of sexual liberation, and I want to make sure we hold up the awareness of the challenges just as much as the importance of the freedom."

Dr. Shemeka Thorpe, PhD, sexuality researcher and educator as well as cofounder of The Minority Sex Report, would agree about the need to widen our thinking of what it means to be sexually liberated, especially as a researcher of Black female sexuality studies. Dr. Thorpe knows that limiting our definitions and restricting labels do not help us. She says, "I feel like we're just constantly trying to follow or to fit into boxes. And the way it works is there's not one size fits all. The most important thing to do is just really give yourself grace. Grace to learn things about yourself, your body and your partner."

Dr. Thorpe's contemporary thought leader, Dr. Tracie Gilbert, created a whole Black sexual epistemology in her PhD program to help explain sexual liberation. For her research and work it was paramount to remove any barriers for Black individuals to be able to engage. In her words, "If we can remove those barriers, that's how we get to liberation. So, we don't necessarily have to use the word 'liberation.' We can [instead] talk about sexiness."

Gilbert adds, "When you ask people to talk about their sexuality, the research tells us that it's very difficult for people. [Instead] when people started telling me about what sexiness was, they were talking about things like confidence and game and being able to do what you want. That is how I get to liberation."

"Sexual empowerment" was the closest phrasing we found to capturing what it means to feel empowered to explore our desires, seek healing for our bodies, and challenge the messages and expectations about who we are.

Whether it's sexiness in the words of Dr. Gilbert or our struggle and path to freedom to echo Dr. Hansen, my biggest hope for you, reader, is that you fill in your own blank of what sexual liberation is to you.

There is no "finish line" to cross or final item to mark off a list.

Decolonizing advocates for embodying rather than intellectualizing things; the focus shifts from "achieving" to creating a freer way of being. We become what we practice and embodying starts with repetition until our body has calibrates a new "default" way of being. Doing the work starts small and moves slowly, with a commitment of leading with curiosity and care. The reflection questions at the end are meant to be in service of that. Be sure to regularly ask yourself new questions too.

Know that these things are meant to be done in community. You will find, just as I did while writing this book, that we are all trying to do this work. Our collective liberation is bound together.

With love,
Mo

REFLECTION QUESTIONS

—

What do you feel is never questioned?

How have you lived in the in-between? What in your experience is only compatible to being understood on a spectrum or nonlinear?

What does building a trusting relationship with your body look like?

How many "puberties" have you gone through? Was puberty a joyful experience for you?

How have you unconsciously gatekept anything related to sex? How have you seen gatekeeping in your own communities around topics of sex and sexuality?

What was your parent(s), guardian(s), or primary caretaker's relationship to sex? How did it impact the entire household? What was your household culture like? And, if at all, did you see that change?

How does white supremacy feel in your body? Where in the body does shame reside for you?

If your body could talk or send you messages, what would be the bulk of those messages? Would your body say you are a good listener when it tries to tell you something?

Has anyone ever shared a sex story (whether theirs or someone else's) without your consent? How did it feel?

Have you shared a sex story without someone's consent? What did it feel like?

Is talking about sex an act of vulnerability for you? Who do you find yourself talking to about sex with the most? What does talking about sex mean to you?

What was your first experience understanding consent, not the actual word but the feeling or experience of consent?

What does it mean for you to explore your sexuality? How have you seen others define it and how has that informed your own understanding?

What is the script you have been taught about sex? Or what is "normal sex" and what is the kind of sex that brings pleasure?

In what ways are you your own medicine? What do you want? Not need, what do you want? Do you think you deserve to get everything you want?

What does pleasure on your own terms mean?

Fill in the blank: sexual liberation is _____.

RESOURCES

————

My learnings have always built and will continue to build on the teachings and work of powerful educators and visionaries, mostly Black, brown, disabled and queer. I do not claim to be the originator of these ideas. We are taught to admire and strive to be those who have "discovered" things and created their own ideas. I have only learned from those who have come before me and who are still with us. In all my work, I cite Black women.

SOCIAL MEDIA ACCOUNTS
Afrosexology
Website: afrosexology.com

Sex Positive Families
Website: https://sexpositivefamilies.com

Radical Families Instagram
@radicalfamiles

The Nap Ministry Instagram
@thenapministry

Instagram Accounts
@tsobthepodcast
@drnikkiknows
@tracieg_the_phd
@scarleteenorg
@theminoritysexreport
@ intersexjusticeproject
@drshemeka
@thefatsextherapist
@sexelducation
@polyamorouswhileasian
@genderfenderbender

DIGITAL COMMUNITY GROUPS
Ethel's Club
ethelsclub.com

BOOKS
Sister Outside by Audre Lorde

Care Work by Leah Lakshmi

Pleasure Activism by Adrienne Maree Brown

We Will Not Cancel Us by Adrienne Maree Brown

The Body Is Not An Apology: The Power of Radical Self Love by Sonya Renee Taylor

A Quick and Easy Guide to Queer & Trans Identities by Mady G & J.R. Zuckerberg

All Boys Aren't Blue by George M. Johnson

The Ultimate Guide to Sex and Disability: For All of Us Who Live with Disabilities, Chronic Pain and Illness by Miriam Kaufman, M.D, Cory Silverberg and Fran Odette

Body Talk: 37 Voices Explore Our Radical Anatomy by Kelly Jensen

A Quick & Easy Guide to Sex & Disability by A. Andrews

The New Queer Conscience by Adam Eli

Beyond the Gender Binary by Alok Vaid-Menon

Pussy Prayers: Sacred & Sensual Rituals for Wild Women of Color by Black Girl Bliss

To My Trans Sisters edited by Charlie Craggs

Becoming Cliterate: Why Organism Equality Matters and How to Get It by Laurie Mintz, Ph.D.

Killing the Black Body: Race, Reproduction and the Meaning of Liberty by Dorothy Roberts

Things No One Will Tell Fat Girls: A Handbook for Unapologetic Living by Jes Baker

My Grandmother's Hands: Racialized Trauma and the Pathway to Mending Our Hearts and Bodies by Resmaa Menakem

PODCASTS
Sensual Self Podcast

Finding Our Way Podcast

The Breathing Room Podcast

Be Well, Sis

ACKNOWLEDGMENTS

To Leah Lakshmi, Adrienne Maree Brown, Audre Lorde and Toni Morrison, thank you for inspiring me to be free.

To my soulmate; thank you for helping me find my way back to myself. You make me proud to be who I am. And I know that your soul and my soul are old friends. I truly do not know what I would do without you in my life.

To the one who knew me since freshman year at the activities fair and has been transcending with me ever since; thank you for our friendship and letting me witness you evolve into the person you are becoming. Thank you for welcoming and honoring my evolution.

To the one who stopped masturbating just to send midnight encouragements and cheer me on during this book journey; you are a force to be reckoned with and I am so excited to see all you do in this big ole world. Thank you for never doubting me.

To the one who lived down the hall and was second to buy the book (or the five books); thank you for being my friend all these years. I am so grateful that we stayed in touch, what a milestone and honor it is to have your support. Sooo, when is yours coming out?

To the one who journaled with me by my side for the last year; thank you for your care, coaching and support. You sat beside me when this book was just a couple of pages and haven't left my side since. You helped me believe in myself as a creative. I will treasure every opportunity to do the same for you.

To the one who made coming out feel like a coming home; thank you for reminding what it feels like to be truly seen. Meeting you has been hands down the best thing ever. BWAM forever.

To the one who lived with me in these past years of becoming and unbecoming; thank you for being there for me. Thank you for all the surprise care packages, the moments of silent understanding, and the unwavering love you have always extended to me.

To the one who was reading *Sister Outsider* when I sat next to them on the bus in 2016; I'm sorry I didn't take your advice and name this book *Mo's Guide to Fucking Right*. Either way, you have a special place in my heart—thank you for always loving me for me.

To the one who first told me how expansive queerness is and how deeply personal the journey of exploring your sexuality can be; thank you for the conversations and questions we had. I hope you see them reflected in this book.

To one of the first people I ever met that could outmatch my energy; thank you darling. Thank you for the help editing and saying everything I needed to hear in the moments I needed to hear them most. You have a gift and it's already been incredible watching you to cultivate it. The world needs more bards like you.

To the one who is always on standby to hype me up and have my back; thank you for doing one of the kindest things anyone has ever done for me. You helped me reconnect to my writing and my 'why' in a time I needed it the most. I can't wait for the roles to be reversed (literally) so you can see just how much I am in your corner.

To my best friend across the globe; cuca—we are friends for a lifetime. I can't wait for our worlds to collide again. MK, perhaps you can be there too?

To Tumise, Eni, Fola, Timi, Simi, Tofunmi & Jimi, I am officially the coolest sibling. Sorry about that.

To my parents, look I wrote a book!

To everyone I interviewed, thank you for being a part of my writing journey. If you did not see your name mentioned in the book, know that I built upon our interview to get to the book you see today. A special thank you to Melissa Carnagey. You are everything my younger self needed. Thank you for doing the work you do.

I'd also like to gratefully acknowledge:

Mrs. Theresa Savage, it was in my periwinkle robe that I finished writing this book. I always feel warm and embraced by your love—no matter how long it has been since I've seen you. Thank you for rallying all of Riverside to support my book journey, and thank you Aunt Shari for your thoughtfulness and the delectable butter mochi.

Lastly, I'd like to thank all of those who pre-ordered a book and by doing so helped make my dream a reality!

Ariel Savage, Sonemani Bitna, Oluremi Akindele, Sarah Panzer, Oluwatumise Asebiomo, Misty Ouyang, Jane Leyva, Arnelle Ansong, Ayoade Balogun, Nikhil A Desai, Xiaowei Wang, Yindi Pei, Alexis Lefft, Camilo Durango, Ashley Burke, Cori Coccia, Kofi Adu, Eva Fernandez Munoz, Juan Fernandez Revuelta, Anna Stone, Isabela Angus, Zoe Mahony, Ashley Song, George Kingston, Jordan Williams, Christopher Tan, Edric Zeng, Nicole Salazar, Vanessa Farley, Darel Scott, Laura Jonsson, Kelsey Urban, Julia Schaepe, Lauren Barineau, Dayonna Tucker, Seth Nosanchuk, Nancy Chang, Rowena Chang, Netta Wang, Michelle Howard, Adeola Lediju, Sojourner Ahebee, Audy Mulia, Kathleen Miller, Katherine Boudreau, Samantha Silverstein, Maria Hong, Carol Tan, Brett Elizabeth Anderson, Leilani Reyes, Daela Taeoalii-Tipton, Katie Gilmartin, Grace Anderson, Misha Perinova, David Exume, Terry Adkins, Dionne Thomas, Nina Rosenblatt, Alka Nath, Kaitlyn Choe, Nineveh O'Connell, Lindy Colaluca-Polling, Sheryl Tecker, Kim Sanchez, Rayna Toyama, Shari Chun, Annie Hansberger, Theresa Savage, Daniel Henry, Mark Ferguson, Jewel Thompson, Melissa Du, Amanda Powell, Isobel Hayne, Mary McCall, Alida Ratteray, Sabrina, Yan Yan, Jas Espinosa, Kelsie Wysong, Raquel

Lane-Arellano, Edith Pan, Selby Sturzenegger, Whitney Lenox, Rachel Wallstrom, Wajih Chaudhry, Adriane Osby, Meghana Rao, Jacob Kuppermann, Joey Friedman, Dylan Cooper, Jam C., Thea Rossman, Nani Friedman, Henry Weller, Nichelle Hall, Nathaniel Arthur Ramos, Vinh Ton, Madison Willcox, Patricia Flores, Sharon Tseng, Marissa Gerchick, Reese Williams, Kimiko Hirota, Stephanie Brito, Adesuwa Agbonile, Zakaria Sharif, Molly Culhane, Renad Abualjamal, Derek McCreight, Sabrina Medler, Kalea Woods, Priya Chatwani, Angie Casarez, Julie Fukunaga, Jesse Calderon, Arkira Chantaratananond, Bryan Aldana, Caleb Martin, Zoe Brownwood, Richard Coca, Jessica Hong, Olivia Arballo-Saenz, Brandon Truong & Eniolufe Asebiomo

APPENDIX

—

PREFACE: A LETTER TO YOU

Blanton, Natalie. "Why Sex Education in the United States Needs an Update and How to Do It." Why Sex Education in The United States Needs an Update and How to do it. Scholars Strategy Network, October 10, 2019. https://scholars.org/contribution/why-sex-education-united-states-needs-update-and-how-do-it.

BREAKING DOWN THE BUZZWORDS

Chung, Jezz. What Does It Mean to Decolonize the Mind (image) December 14, 2020 (@jezzchung) https://www.instagram.com/p/CIymclOhYsH/.

Cullors, Patrisse. "Q&A: Nap Ministry's Tricia Hersey Talks Rest and Racial Justice." Q&A: Nap Ministry's Tricia Hersey talks rest and racial justice. Prism, March 22, 2021. https://prism-reports.org/2020/09/03/qa-nap-ministrys-tricia-hersey-talks-rest-and-racial-justice/.

Crossman, Ashley. "What Is Social Oppression?" ThoughtCo. https://www.thoughtco.com/social-oppression-3026593 (accessed May 12, 2021).

Jones, Kenneth, and Tema Okun. "White Supremacy Culture from Dismantling Racism: A Workbook for Social Change Groups," 2001. https://www.dismantlingracism.org.

Taylor, Sonya Renee. *Body Is Not an Apology: A Guide to Radical Self-Love.* Berrett-Koehler Publishers, Incorporated, 2018.

Price, Devon. *Laziness Does Not Exist.* S.l.: ATRIA BOOKS, 2021.

Wolfe, Patrick. "Settler Colonialism and the Elimination of the Native." *Journal of Genocide Research* 8, no. 4 (2006): 387-409.

SEX POSITIVITY AND WHY IT NEEDS TO BE DECOLONIZED

Alexander, Apryl A. "Sex for All: Sex Positivity and Intersectionality in Clinical and Counseling Psychology." *Journal of Black Sexuality and Relationships* 6, no. 1 (2019): 49-72. doi:10.1353/bsr.2019.0015.

Glover, Cameron. "Wild Flower Sex Is a Lesson in White Abuse of Power." *Wear Your Voice*, September 13, 2019. https://www.wearyourvoicemag.com/wild-flower-sex-white-abuse-power/.

Alex Iantaffi. 2012, White Privilege in Sex and Relationship Therapy, Sexual and Relationship Therapy, 27:2, 99-102, DOI: 10.1080/14681994.2012.708196).

Kauanui, J. Kēhaulani. "'A structure, not an event': Settler Colonialism and Enduring Indigeneity." *Lateral* 5, no. 1 (2016): 5-1.

Meenadchi. *Decolonizing Non-Violent Communication: A Workbook*. Co-Conspirator Press, 2020.

Mogilevsky, Miri. "10 Things Sex Positivity Is Not," Everyday Feminism, August 23, 2016, https://everydayfeminism.com/2016/08/10-things-sex-positivity-is-not/.

SEX SOCIALIZATION AS A VEHICLE FOR SOCIAL CHANGE

DePasse, Emily L. "Sexelducation: Emily L. DEPASSE." SexELDucation | EMILY L. DEPASSE. Accessed June 19, 2021. https://www.emilydepasse.com/.

Johnson, George M. *All Boys Aren't Blue*. Random House UK, 2021.

Lorde, Audre. "Uses of the Erotic." Essay. In *Sister Outsider Essays and Speeches*, 57. Berkeley, Calif: Ten Speed Press, 2016.

Mosher, Chad M. "Historical Perspectives of Sex Positivity: Contributing to a New Paradigm Within Counseling Psychology." The Counseling Psychologist 45, no. 4 (May 2017): 487–503. https://doi.org/10.1177/0011000017713755.

Shah, Courtney Q. "Race, Gender, and Sex Education in 20th-Century America." In *Oxford Research Encyclopedia of American History*. 2017.

"Sexual Information and Education Council of the United States (SIECUS)." National Sexual Violence Resource Center. Accessed November 19, 2020. https://www.nsvrc.org/organizations/103.

Tatter, Grace. "Sex Education That Goes beyond Sex." Harvard Graduate School of Education, November 28, 2018. https://www.gse.harvard.edu/news/uk/18/11/sex-education-goes-beyond-sex.

Vaid-Menon, Alok. *Beyond the Gender Binary*. New York, New York: Penguin, 2020.

SILENCE AS THE TOOL OF THE OPPRESSOR

Carnagey, Melissa Pintor. *Sex Positive Talks to Have with Kids: A Guide to Raising Sexually Healthy, Informed, Empowered Young People*. United States: Sex Positive Families, 2020.

Ford, Jessie V., Esther Corona Vargas, Itor Finotelli Jr, J. Dennis Fortenberry, Eszter Kismödi, Anne Philpott, Eusebio Rubio-Aurioles, and Eli Coleman. "Why pleasure matters: Its global relevance for sexual health, sexual rights and wellbeing." *International Journal of Sexual Health* 31, no. 3 (2019): 217-230.

Jaccard, James, Tonya Dodge, and Patricia Dittus. "Parent⊠adolescent communication about sex and birth control: A conceptual framework." *New directions for child and adolescent development* 2002, no. 97 (2002): 9-42.

Markham, Christine M., Donna Lormand, Kari M. Gloppen, Melissa F. Peskin, Belinda Flores, Barbara Low, and Lawrence

Duane House. "Connectedness as a predictor of sexual and reproductive health outcomes for youth." *Journal of adolescent health* 46, no. 3 (2010): S23-S41.

Rakovec-Felser, Zlatka. "Domestic violence and abuse in intimate relationship from public health perspective." *Health psychology research* 2, no. 3 (2014).

"Talking with Your Teens about Sex: Going beyond 'The Talk.'" Talking with Your Teens about Sex: Going Beyond "the Talk." Centers for Disease Control and Prevention, November 21, 2019. https://www.cdc.gov/healthyyouth/protective/factsheets/talking_teens.htm.

NOISE FROM THOSE IN POWER

Brown Brené. *Daring Greatly: How the Courage to Be Vulnerable Transforms the Way We Live, Love, Parent, and Lead*. London: Penguin Life, 2015.

COMPROMISE IS COLONIAL

Carnagey, Melissa Pintor. *Sex Positive Talks to Have with Kids: A Guide to Raising Sexually Healthy, Informed, Empowered Young People*. United States: Sex Positive Families, 2020.

Kirlew, Chloe, Crucial Consent: A OnePeopleTO Conversation Series: Healthcare Consent (@thereiqueer) https://www.instagram.com/p/CKzmjzxgGic/.

Price, Joan. "Author, Speaker, and Advocate for Ageless Sexuality." Joan Price, June 25, 2021. https://joanprice.com/.

PLEASURE IS NOT A LUXURY

Brown, Adrienne Maree. *Pleasure Activism the Politics of Feeling Good*. Chico: AK Press, 2019.

Johnson, Lacey. "No, Being Sex Positive Doesn't Mean You Want to Spend All Day in the Bedroom." Oprah Daily, March 26, 2021. https://www.oprahdaily.com/life/relationships-love/a30028506/sex-positive-meaning/.

Saah, Dalychia. "Meet Dalychia." Afrosexology. Accessed September 29, 2021. https://www.afrosexology.com/dalychia.

www.SiteWizard.co.uk. "Declaration on Sexual Pleasure." World Association for Sexual Health (WAS), October 16, 2019. https://worldsexualhealth.net/declaration-on-sexual-pleasure/.

Thomas, Adele. "Stolen People on Stolen Land: Decolonizing While Black." Racebaitr.com, May 24, 2016. https://racebaitr.com/2016/05/24/stolen-people-stolen-land/.

PLEASURE IS A MEASURE OF FREEDOM

Biko, Steve, and Aelred Stubbs. *I Write What I like: A Selection of His Writings*. London: Heinemann, 1982.

Fuller, Kristen MD. "Body Positivity vs. Body Neutrality." Body Positivity vs. Body Neutrality. Verywell Mind, May 28, 2021. https://www.verywellmind.com/body-positivity-vs-body-neutrality-5184565.

Taylor, Sonya Renee. *Body Is Not an Apology: A Guide to Radical Self-Love*. Berrett-Koehler Publishers, Incorporated, 2018.

Piepzna-Samarasinha, Leah Lakshmi. *Care Work: Dreaming Disability Justice*. Vancouver, BC: Arsenal Pulp Press, 2019.

QUEERING SEX POSITIVITY

Capire, and Words by Tica MorenoReviewed by Helena ZelicTranslated from Portuguese by Aline Scátola. "#Feministschool: Women and Gender-Nonconforming Bodies in Resistance." Capire, May 23, 2021. https://capiremov.org/en/experience/feministschool-women-and-gender-nonconforming-bodies-in-resistance/.

Price, Devon. *Laziness Does Not Exist*. S.l.: ATRIA BOOKS, 2021.

Wynne, Griffin. "Compulsory Heterosexuality: What to Know About the Term 'Comphet' You've Seen on Tiktok." MSN. Cosmopolitan, August 5, 2021. https://www.msn.com/en-in/lifestyle/relationships/compulsory-heterosexuality-what-to-know-about-the-term-comphet-youve-seen-on-tiktok/amp/ar-AAMWHny.

Vaid-Menon, Alok. *Beyond the Gender Binary*. New York, New York: Penguin, 2020.

LIBERATION: A CUSTOM FIT

Bennett, Dan, and Aliya Arman. "Why the Sex Positivity Movement Has a Long Way to Go." lappthebrand. lappthebrand, August 17, 2018. https://www.lappthebrand.com/blogs/perspectives/why-the-sex-positivity-movement-has-a-long-way-to-go.

Whitney, Ev'Yan. "Sensual Self Podcast." Ev'Yan Whitney, Sexuality Doula®. Accessed October 19, 2021. https://www.evyanwhitney.com/podcast.

Made in the USA
Las Vegas, NV
29 March 2022

46498801R00075